# Wise
# Child

HAY
HOUSE

# Wise Child

A Practical Guide to Raising Kids with Sensitive Hearts and Smart Souls in a World They Were Reborn to Save

## AMY MOLLOY

*Founder of LightWriter Media*

**HAY HOUSE LLC**
Carlsbad, California • New York City
London • Sydney • New Delhi

# Praise for
# Wise Child

*'A paradigm-shifting book, which will transform your family dynamic.'*
— Intuitive, energy healer and speaker, Dana Childs

*'Our children are earth's real spiritual leaders. This is the roadmap to parent them.'*
— David Stevens, Australia's leading Clairvoyant and Spiritual Medium

*'If we want a better world, we have to parent in new ways. This book will tell you how.'*
– Peter Smith, founder, Institute for Quantum Consciousness

*Published in Australia by:*
Hay House Australia Publishing Pty Ltd, www.hayhouse.com.au
P.O. Box 7201, Alexandria NSW 2015


*Design by* Rhett Nacson
*Typeset by* Bookhouse, Sydney
*Edited by* Maggie Hamilton
*Author Photo by* Exist Images

**Tradepaper ISBN:** 9781401997571
**E-book ISBN:** 9781401999056

10 9 8 7 6 5 4 3 2 1
1st edition, March 2025


The authorized representative in the EU for product safety and compliance is Penguin Random House Ireland, Morrison Chambers, 32 Nassau Street, Dublin D02 YH68,

Ireland. https://eu-contact.penguin.ie

*To my three, P, Z and H.*

*And to all the world's children.*
*This one's for you.*

# Contents

## PART 3: REPARENTING YOURSELF

# Introduction
## Starting Again

*Once you look back, you'll never go back ...*

▷ There's something wrong with my baby.' This is what I would have told you if I had the courage to say it aloud during the first year of my son's life. I was not a first-time mother, so I thought I was prepared for the challenges of a newborn. But, from the moment our son was born, he seemed different: unsettled, disrupted and, often, impossible to soothe.

As a mother, I knew enough to know that children mirror their parent's emotions so, of course, I blamed myself for his symptoms: an inability to sleep, sensitivity to noise and crowds, the cough he couldn't shake, his unexplainable rash and a general sense that ... he just didn't want to be 'here'.

By the time my son was 14 months old, I was depleted and I'd run out of coping mechanisms. At the time, I wasn't new to the world of inner-work and spiritual healing. Since my dad had been diagnosed with cancer when I was a teenager and begun his own healing experiment, I had been piggy-backing on my parent's spiritual journey. I learnt how to meditate when I was 17 years old and, throughout the challenges in my life, which included my first-husband's death when I was 23, I'd supplemented psychotherapy with all kinds of complementary therapies.

I'd been visiting the same spiritual healer, Yvonne, in England since my early twenties, even after I emigrated from London to Sydney, Australia. Over the years, we'd explored my mind-body-soul connection and I'd even dipped my toe into past life regression to find a solution to the eating disorder, which I carried through my teenage years and twenties.

But the focus of that healing had always been me. After becoming a mother, I never thought to investigate the past lives of my children. (Why would I?) That was until one memorable session with Yvonne when, after stumbling off a 28-hour flight with a toddler and a baby, I sat crying on her sofa. Did I really have it in me to parent these children, especially the more sensitive of the two souls? As always, Yvonne told me to trust my inner knowing and then we began our session.

An hour later, I walked out of that appointment with a complete understanding of my son's past life—and a new blueprint for how to parent him. In that session, I received a full download of who he'd been, why he chose to come into the world again now and why he struggled with certain 'modern' stimuli.

From that day forward, I stopped parenting him with the same cookie-cutter strategies that had worked so well with his sister. I realised that this child, like all children, is a complex soul with their own preferences, desires and triggers—the result of many experiences during many lifetimes. It felt like I'd been handed a secret key to his being.

Perhaps you're feeling sceptical, and I don't blame you. During my career as a journalist, editor and content creator, I've written thousands of articles, blogs, pods and books. But writing the introduction for this book gave me severe writer's block. How could I put this metaphysical concept into words in a way that didn't sound too *out there*? There isn't really a way, so I'm just leaning into it.

My name is Amy Molloy and I'm a 'Past Life Parent'. When it comes to raising my three children, aged three, five and six, I have discovered that it's not enough to observe how they feel on the day and to react to it. I also need to look backwards—way backwards; to remember where they've come from and who they were, even before they landed in this body. This is what I've learnt from past life parenting so far.

 ▷ My middle child, my son, was once a great healer, long ago. Before I gave birth to him, he hadn't reincarnated for hundreds of years. This is why he arrived early and dramatically; why his birth wasn't conventional; why he was so unsettled for the first year of his life. The modern world was a dramatic adjustment for his energy.

 ▷ My eldest daughter, who is now six, was once a pagan herbalist. She woke before dawn every single morning to walk through fog-covered fields, gathering nuts and berries for herbal medicines. She also had a special place in her heart for animals. It's the reason she and her dad, an environmental scientist, have such a special connection.

 ▷ My youngest daughter, now three-years-old, was born during the Covid lockdown out of choice—her choice. Like every child born during the height of the pandemic, she knew exactly what she was doing. She chose those circumstances to make her entrance. (This means, I've never had to feel guilty or to worry that she can't cope with these circumstances.)

I won't tell you how I know all this right now—that will come in later chapters. But, getting a glimpse into the former lives of my children has transformed how I feel as their mother; reducing stress, increasing acceptance and enjoyment, and removing the need to compare my kids to other people's.

And I'm not alone! When I started researching this book and began talking about it openly, even my sceptical friends seemed to sit up and take notice. One mum, a lawyer, told me, 'My son tells me that he can remember his 'other life.' He even talks about his 'second parents''. Another mum, an accountant, revealed, her daughter talks about her grandmother, who died three years earlier, and how she is 'now a little girl again.' (As you'll read later, it is possible to speak to a deceased person, who has also been reincarnated. This part is mind-blowing.)

For this book, I have deep-dived into the past life space. I interviewed past life experts across the world, including regressionists, hypnotherapists and mediums. Many have backgrounds in traditional psychotherapy, medicine and education, and they're just as surprised to be talking about past lives as I am.

Yes, we could write it off as childish nonsense or the product of an active imagination, but what if it's more than that? We can keep searching for answers to the stress of parenting outside our family—or we could start to listen to the wisdom that's coming out of the mouths of our babes.

## ▷ What Our 'Comeback Kids' Want us to Know

The West is coming late to the whole past lives outlook. It's a concept that over a billion people on the planet (in India, Bali, Nepal and beyond) already know about and integrate into their way of living. What is new and exciting is how parents in the West are now catching up—and learning to use this powerful knowledge to parent in a new way.

Here are just some of the gifts that past life parenting can give mums, dads, educators, grandparents and carers:

▷ An instant remedy to the stress and overwhelm of modern caregiving.

▷ A new way of understanding their child's make-up and innate characteristics.

▷ A third option when it comes to nature versus nurture.

▷ A new approach to issues around sleep, phobias and physical symptoms.

▷ A new appreciation for those kids who are labelled 'difficult' and 'problematic'.

▷ A new attitude to childhood trauma and hope for kids who are born into difficult circumstances.

▷ A new relationship with time.

▷ A new relationship with death.

▷ A new way of talking to your child about love, loss and separation.

▷ A new approach to neurodiversity and celebrating neurodivergence.

▷ An instant boost of confidence, both in your child's capabilities and your own abilities as a parent.

▷ Plus, scripts, strategies and exercises for teaching kids how to protect their energy, reduce anxiety, trust their intuition and cosmically heal as a family.

Eight months into writing this book, my own mother—who can be my harshest critic—said, 'I've seen such a change in you, Amy. You seem to really *enjoy* your children now.' I knew exactly what she meant, because I had felt the shift too. I had gone from enduring motherhood to enjoying it; from resisting it to relishing it. Of course, there are still moments when my kids set off alarm bells in my nervous system. But I love being around them—and I love who I am when I'm with them.

Not only am I more capable and compassionate when my children are struggling, but I can see the mutual benefits of our relationship. As a mum, it can feel like you're doing everything for everyone else. It can be exhausting when everyone is always looking to you for solutions and answers (and to make them a sandwich). Past life parenting rebalances the burden.

Let's assume, your kids know far more than you think they do. Now, you can start listening to them and turning to *them* for guidance. Of course, you have to pick your circumstances. (Your kindergartener probably won't do your tax return.) But, I love turning to my children for their wisdom and intuition. What do they need to feel supported in this moment? Why do *they* think they feel scared? If they were Mummy, what would they do?

If indeed this concept is correct, and our children have been here before—and even remember it—then it can bring great comfort and empowerment for parents. You don't need to know all the answers. Your children know far more than you think they do, and it's okay and even wise to trust them.

## ▷ A Radical Approach to Parenting

My advice as you traverse this book is to remain open and curious, and make everything you read a conversation-starter. Talk about it with your partner; talk about it with your kids; talk about it with your own parents (and your therapist!). Notice how it feels in your body and your soul. Yes, we're going to talk about souls, so get comfortable with it!

Like all metaphysical concepts, there isn't concrete evidence. In fact, I'm not here to tell you what's true. As I say to my kids when we talk about death, 'Nobody knows for sure, that's what makes death the greatest adventure.' But I do believe, we're doing ourselves a disservice by not having conversations about life, death and afterlife. So many of us spend our lives running away from the D-word, even though it's going to happen to everyone. Let's normalise having deep, enriching conversations about death—and rebirth—so that we don't raise children who are haunted by mortality. I dream that my children are so accepting of the circle of life, they never have to engage in toxic behaviour to escape it.

The idea of past life parenting may seem new to you, especially if you live in the West. It was new for me when I began and, even 62,000 words later, I'm still learning. The point of this book is to see how it makes you feel and, possibly, to embrace a new parenting blueprint.

For our children to thrive in this world, we need a radically progressive approach to parenting. We need to break the paradigm, which places parents above children in the hierarchy of importance—and wisdom. It's time to realise, the latest generation of children have been born with the wisdom of the universe in their souls. Now, we, as millennial parents, have a choice: do we repress that knowledge, or do we value it?

Our parents had this chance with us, millennial children. Many of us born with an incredible knowing and inner wisdom. Unfortunately, it was a different time, and parenting trends still leaned towards criticism and harsh discipline. Look back to how you remember feeling as a child (especially in the years before your seventh birthday). Did you move through the world with a greater confidence and deeper knowing, before the world told you that what you felt and thought didn't have worth?

We missed an opportunity with us—let's not do it again with Gen Alpha and younger.

## ▷ Tuned-in Parents, Trusting Children

Writing this book was more than a project for me. It also became a personal experiment. It allowed me to embrace my children, to accept the limits of my parenting, to trust our family's collective journey and even to heal my relationship with my own parents. And it can do the same for you too.

It's a big promise, I know. The truth is, you might get to the end of this book and say, 'I'm just not buying into it.' But I am confident that will not be the same person as when you started reading it. Somewhere along the way, you will read a paragraph that sticks with you; an idea that keeps you awake at night, which you can't help sharing with anyone who will listen. That sticky paragraph is the one you need the most. It's the reason you picked up this book in the first place.

For now, I just want you to think of past life parenting as an extension of your regular parenting. It's business-as-usual ... but with a bonus. When you'd usually run out of patience, tolerance, compassion, energy and faith, past life parenting has the power to extend all your inner resources and capabilities. We'll go into exactly how, I promise. For now, I just want you to feel open to possibilities.

This book isn't about proving a theory or telling you what to believe. It's about finding a way to trust your child's wisdom and needs, whilst still having clear boundaries and making safe decisions. (Sorry, we can't have ice-cream for dinner, even if your past life persona is craving it!)

This book isn't about believing one thing without doubt. It's about challenging our hierarchical idea of parenting—that parents should know everything and children know nothing—in order to find sweet relief, and create tuned-in parents and trusting children.

There's a huge relief when you realise that a parent doesn't need all the answers—and a child has more answers than we think they do. Plus, it makes life a lot more fun.

Amy x

## ▷ A Message for the Exhausted Parent

If you're a parent in the trenches of sleep regression or school refusal, even thinking about reading this book might feel like a mission. I wish I could tell you to just skip to the end, but I do believe that there's something in every chapter that can help you.

Parenting like this can be an energy boost. I know it can feel easier to parent from the old paradigm, because it's been ingrained into us. But I found that, by the end of writing this book, I had more energy, more mental freedom and vitality.

Of course, I still feel exhausted after a sleepless night with my three-year-old or a turbulent weekend of sibling arguments. But I can also regain my equilibrium more easily and that has transformed my energy supplies. Plus, my relationship with my husband has gotten stronger. (Even our sex life has improved thanks to an 'Ancestral Forgiveness' exercise that I'll share in a later chapter.)

So, I do urge you to stick with this book. Yes, even on the days you're depleted. My advice is to find a couple of mum (or dad) friends and to read it together for motivation. Start a WhatsApp group to chat about the chapters that stick with you and make it a collective experience. (Like all things in motherhood, past life parenting is even better in a village.)

If you can, carve out ten minutes each day to read a chapter. I kept them short to make them parent-friendly. My hope is that, by the end of this book, you'll remember your own capabilities, ditch some past life baggage, and rediscover the joy of parenting like I did.

## ▷ **Five Day Past Life Parenting Plan**

If you are intrigued to try Past Life Parenting in your own family, I have created a Five-Day Past Life Parenting Plan, which you can access for free on my website, *amymolloy.com.au/pastlifeparenting*. Over five days, I'll share key ideas from this book, packaged into practical, impactful steps, which will fit into even the busiest parenting schedule. On my website, I also share bonus resources to accompany this book, including worksheets, cheat sheets and meditations for you and your whole family.

# PART 1: PARENTING FROM THE PAST

*If you die in one dimension, you'll come back in another dimension, but you're not completely the same. I know, it's hard for your generation to understand. Mum, I'm not afraid of death. I live in full acceptance. You should know, there is nothing to be afraid of.*

*Alex, aged 10.*

# Chapter 1:
# **Generation Reincarnation**

*The point of life is to rebirth yourself again and again.*

▷ I can't possibly write about past life parenting without mentioning the work of the Division of Perceptual Studies (DOPS) at the University of Virginia. A research group dedicated to the 'rigorous evaluation of empirical evidence for extraordinary human experiences', the primary focus of DOPS is investigating the possibility of consciousness surviving physical death. For the past sixty years, 'children who remember past lives' has been a major area of their investigations.

Currently, Doctor Jim Tucker is the director of DOPS. A child psychiatrist and professor of psychiatry and neurobehavioral sciences, he is, by his own admission, a natural sceptic. It was his wife who encouraged him to apply for a job at DOPS, under the previous director, Doctor Ian Stevenson. Since then, Dr. Tucker has led a team, that travels the world speaking to children who appear to remember past life memories. Currently, they have a database of over 2,500 case studies. On the website for DOPS, they list examples of statements that a child may make[1]:

▷ 'You're not my mummy/daddy.'
▷ 'I have another mummy/daddy.'

▷ 'When I was big, I ... (used to have blue eyes/had a car, etc).'

▷ 'That happened before I was in mummy's tummy.'

▷ 'I have a wife/husband/children.'

▷ 'I used to ... (drive a truck/live in another town, etc).'

▷ 'I died ... (in a car accident/after I fell, etc).'

▷ 'Remember when I ... (lived in that other house/was your daddy, etc).'

The challenge, of course, is proving the truth in these statements. Is it fantasy or a memory? Can the child's statement be verified? Does their story match someone who has lived and died in the past? 'Nothing is indisputable,' says Dr. Tucker, in a video posted on YouTube. 'But there is certainly very solid evidence, children from all over the world have memories of a past life, which can be verified to match somebody who did live and die in the past.'[2]

Some of the cases are too 'weak' to prove and then there are jaw-dropping examples, which the DOPS have gone to great lengths to investigate. These include, but are not limited to:

▷ **The World War II pilot.** At the age of two, American child, James Leininger began having intense nightmares of a plane crash. He then described being an American pilot who was killed when his plane was shot down by the Japanese. He gave details that included the name of an American aircraft carrier, the first and last name of a friend who was on the ship with him, and a location and other specifics about the fatal crash. His parents discovered a close correspondence between James's statements and the death of a World War II pilot named James Huston.

▷ **The Hollywood Actor.** When Ryan Hammons was four years old, he began directing imaginary movies. He told his parents that he recalled a life as an actor called Marty Martyn, working in Hollywood. After his curious mother took some books about Hollywood out of the library, Ryan pointed to one of the photos and said, 'That's me.' Working with a Hollywood archivist, Doctor Tucker and his team were able to verify that 55 of Ryan's statements matched Marty Martyn's life, including the fact he died of a heart attack. (Ryan would wake up screaming in the night, telling his parents he remembered his 'heart exploding in Hollywood.')

As with all of these cases, nothing can be entirely proven. There are plenty of alternative theories, says Dr. Tucker, including that the knowledge was acquired through 'normal means' (such as reading a newspaper article). There is also the mystical concept of 'thought bundles', also referred to as 'thought pools' (the idea that we emit thought bundles before we die that can get 'attached' to another person). In multiple interviews, Dr. Tucker has said that reincarnation is 'the most obvious explanation'.

Hundreds of parents contact the DOPs every year to share, and hopefully verify, their child's past life memories. Their research has showed some interesting patterns. Children who remember past lives clearly seem to have 'come back' quickly. (In the case studies they have examined, the average interval from the death of the previous person to the birth of the child is 4.5 years). Often, a child's memory of a past life fades before the age of seven, although some children do remember it when they're older. (Very rarely does it continue into adolescence.)

It is also common for a child to have a birthmark, which appears to be related to an injury in their past life or the way in which they died. In his book, *Return to Life,* Dr. Tucker writes: 'A third of the cases from India include birthmarks or birth defects that are thought to correspond to wounds on the previous personalities, with 18 per cent of those including medical records that confirm the match.'

The subjects of these cases have been found all over the world, including Europe and North America. For the past 20 years, Dr. Jim Tucker has focused mainly on cases found in the United States. These statements can occur in families with a belief in reincarnation or in families where the idea of reincarnation has never been considered.

On the DOPS website, Dr. Tucker offers advice for parents: 'When children talk about a past life, parents are sometimes unsure how to respond,' he writes. 'We recommend that parents be open to what their children are reporting. Some of the children show a lot of emotional intensity regarding these issues, and parents should be respectful in listening just as they are with other subjects that their children bring up.'

The DOPS focuses on 'spontaneous' past life memories, so it's better not to quiz your kid for details. 'We do think it's fine to ask general, open-ended questions such as 'Do you remember anything else?", adds Dr. Tucker. 'It is certainly fine to empathise with a child's statement ('That must have been scary').'

In their experience, parents often find children's claims to remember previous life more remarkable than do the children.

▷ **Past Life Pop-outs**

As a parent, I know what I did when I first heard about this research. Straight away, I went through a mental inventory of everything my children have ever said, searching for evidence of a past life memory. Is that what you're doing right now? Does anything 'unusual' spring to mind?

Thankfully, it can be more subtle than a 'death day' memory. Has your child ever had a reoccurring dream? An unexplained phobia? Have they ever come out with a statement that wows you with its wisdom?

Let's be honest, our kids say a lot of things and, sometimes, we have to tune out for the sake of our eardrums. However, once you start tuning into your kids 'past life pop-outs', you might be amazed by what you hear and what they're trying to tell you.

This is where past life parenting can become fun, and even healing, for parents. In between the endless conversations about Pokémon and all those fart jokes, you can get hit with a piece of knowledge that transforms your entire perspective. It's one of the reasons I tell my counselling clients to keep a journal of 'amazing things my kids say', because they often provide incredible wisdom and it's easy to forget them.

One of my clients, an amazing entrepreneur from Europe, had lost her mum to cancer and was dealing with health anxiety. One night, her 10-year-old son had something to share with her. 'If you die in one dimension, you'll come back in another dimension, but you're not completely the same,' he said. 'I know, it's hard for your generation to understand. Mum, I'm not afraid of death. I live in full acceptance. You should know, there is nothing to be afraid of.' These are the moments of clarity that we should celebrate and share with each other.

I'm grateful to have a small group of amazing mum friends who truly see my children for everything they are. Yes, we message each other when our kids drive us bananas. But we also message each other when they leave us in awe. Both sides of the motherhood equation are welcome. Sometimes, it's easier to see the wisdom in our friends' children—that's a great starting point for past life parenting.

My friend, Jane, who you'll meet in a later chapter has an incredibly 'old soul' in her 13-year-old son. Every time I meet him, he hits me with an amazing knowledge-bomb. One of my youngest daughter's friends, Emily, has such an amazing essence that every time she cuddles me, I feel like I've come out of a reiki session. She is a healer, just born that way. Have you met kids like this? Have you told their parents how you feel about them? If not, why not?

The research team from The University of Virginia has been exploring this topic for sixty years, but now is the moment it's going mainstream. Why? Because it's becoming more acceptable to celebrate our children—including their magical, mystical memories. As I write this, parents are taking to social media to share their past life pop-outs—and their kid's memoires are going viral.

## ▷ Coming Back is the New Black

At the time of writing this book, social media is abundant with stories of kids who seem to recall past life memories—you just have to search for them. As I type this, there are 199.7 million posts on TikTok under the category of 'past lives', and a large sub-category of them involve children.

The stories include a four-year-old, who pointed at a photo of the Twin Towers and told her mum that she had worked there. One day, the building got extremely hot, and she jumped out of a window 'like a bird.' Another little boy, Zander, told his mum that he had died in the ocean trying to save his grandmother who was swimming. He was also called Zander in that life, he said. His mum, who shared the story in a TikTok post, said the name had come to her in a dream before she had found out that she was pregnant[3].

The online forum, Reddit is also a hot-bed for past life stories, including a selection of anecdotes curated on a post titled, *'Parents, share spooky past life memories your kid has uttered.*[4] The responses included:

> ▷ 'My youngest (4-5) would talk about how warm and cosy she was in my belly, how cold and scary it was to be born, and how the hardest part was that she "used to know everything" but now she "doesn't know anything".'

> ▷ 'When my son was three, he told his mom that he was a cosmonaut the last time he was a grown-up. Not an astronaut, the Russian version. We're 99 per cent certain he hadn't heard the word before.'

> ▷ 'My daughter asked me, "Remember my fancy hat," and when I said no, she said, "Yeah, before I was dead, I used to work in a bank. I saved my money and bought a hat in a round box. I was on the bus and a man almost sat on it. Then the bus crashed, and I died." She was about three and totally casual about it.'

> ▷ 'My middle son used to talk about having a different mom before me. He would bring it up randomly and only ever got a bit emotional when he would tell me that when he was with her, he never got to grow up. He said he chose me to be his mum this time because I would let him grow up and get old.'

A lot of parents share these anecdotes out of curiosity, amazement and, in many cases, confusion and bewilderment. They tend to believe their children, but they're also at a loss. What should they do with this information now that their child has shared it?

We feel the same when our children tell us they're terrified of the dentist or don't want to go to school that day. On one level, we're grateful they felt safe enough to put their thoughts and feelings into words. But, now what do we do? Don't worry, this book aims to bridge that disconnect.

If your child has said—or says—something unusual, which feels adjacent to a past life memory, the first thing to do is avoiding panicking. This is not an emergency. In fact, take a moment to breathe and see it as a gift. They're sharing something with you that feels intimate to them. They want you to get to know them. They also know, on some level, that if you know them—really know them—you can also better support them.

Many of us have experienced those incredible moments as a parent. When you're lying in your kid's bed, whispering them to sleep, and they decide to open up to you. You feel their warm little body relax against yours as they release a memory or a fear, or a thought that's been consuming them. In past life parenting, this is ten-fold, because they may have been carrying a memory for a century.

There is nothing scary you need to do right now. Simply pay attention, get curious and acknowledge that your child is a complex soul—and you have the pleasure to know them.

## ▷ Believing Outside the Box

It is possible that you've already read something in this book that clashes with your own belief systems. If that's the case, don't worry. There is a surprising amount of cross-over between reincarnation and different belief systems and, if you can open your mind to believing outside your traditional box, then you might surprise yourself.

Nearly nine out of 10 Americans say that they have at least one belief that loosely falls into the category of 'new age' spiritualty, including reincarnation and karma.[5] In Australia, one in five people believe in a mixture of spiritual beliefs from major religions. One in four believe in 'the inward journey of discovering the inner person.'[6]

To me, this is great news—for us, individually, and us as a society. I was raised with what I call a 'mixed-religious upbringing'. I went to Catholic school from the age of five to 16 and, for a large part of that, I went to church every week. However, when I was a teenager and my dad was diagnosed with stage five cancer, he began to see a spiritual healer—my spiritual healer, Yvonne. During this process, he began to follow Hinduism and Buddhism, and began studying with Brahma Kumaris—the largest spiritual organisation in the world that is led by women.

As a result, my spiritual upbringing was incredibly diverse and rich, and I think it only benefited me. When we believe in one belief system—and decide that's the 'right' way—we cut ourselves off from the rich teachings of the others. I am happy for my children to experience a 'pick 'n' mix' of beliefs—and hopefully they'll avoid any doctrine that is hateful or restrictive.

Traditionally, there are three main religions which, generally speaking, encourage a belief in reincarnation or rebirth: Hinduism, Buddhism and Jainism. However, there are some differences in teachings.

In Hinduism, it is believed that all life goes through a cycle of birth, life, death and rebirth. At death, many Hindus believe the soul is carried by a subtle body into a new physical body which can be a human or non-human form (an animal or divine being).

This is where Buddhist teachings differ, because, in Buddhism, nothing is permanent—including your soul. The Buddha taught that 'rebirth' is better understood as the action of a life continuing in a new life, or the transferral of energy.

To be honest, in the first draft of this book, I had a far more comprehensive comparison of religious teachings. However, there are plenty of amazing books and resources out there that outline these belief systems, if you are interested.

I also think it's important to be progressive, especially when it comes to principles that help people understand the surrounding world and their role in it. So, with respect to all the teachings of the past, in this book, I've chosen to interview very modern-day healers, intuits and mediums. What do they think we need to know about rebirth today? What do we need to realise about reincarnation that we've never realised before? What are they sensing, channelling, downloading and de-coding?

If you want a book that's going to tell you what to believe in, this isn't it. If you're anyone who wants to believe that life is cyclical, get curious! In a world that often makes no sense, it feels okay to me to believe in reincarnation in your own way, outside the rulebook of one set religion.

According to research, even being open to reincarnation can have a lot of emotional benefits. One study published in the *Journal of Loss and Trauma* found that a belief in reincarnation helped the parents of fallen soldiers to feel less helpless and hopeless[7]. In contemporary Japan, a Buddhist ritual called *mizuko kuyo*—a water child memorial service—is helping parents from all cultural backgrounds to ease the pain of miscarriage, stillbirth and abortion.[8]

There is a reason a lot of people begin to explore reincarnation during a challenging period in their life, especially after someone they love has passed away. Can you imagine a time in your future when believing in rebirth could bring you huge comfort: if your child gets sick; if you get sick; as your children grow; as your parents age; on the fateful day when you have to say goodbye to one of your children or a loved one for this lifetime. We all know, that day is coming one day.

For me, rebirth is not a belief system I was born into. It's a concept that I decided to choose, which is motivated, I'm sure, by my early experiences with loss and heartbreak, and the need to find a deeper level of faith and acceptance.

In the famous case of James Leininger, the World War II pilot, his father was a devout Christian who didn't believe in past lives ... until his son started remembering one. When his dad gave an interview to the religious newspaper, *The Christian Post* he said, 'I am a Christian and this only re-affirmed the strength of my faith. It's a new reality.'[9]

In a YouTube interview in which he discussed the James Leininger case, Dr Tucker shared: 'In that case, the family incorporated the belief into their overall religious belief. It doesn't challenge their original belief, it just adds to it.'[10]

He adds, 'It can be comforting to think, we may get to have more experiences with our loved ones. It can be comforting to know, we hopefully get another shot at trying to make ourselves better.'

## Chapter 1 ▷ Thinking Points

▷ Has your child ever come out with a story which could, in hindsight, have been a past life memory?

▷ Have they ever had a dream which sounds very real, perhaps linked to a different point in history?

▷ How could the idea of rebirth fit into your own belief system, even if it means 'adding' onto your own traditional beliefs?

▷ What could be gained from being open to the idea that life may begin again?

# Chapter 2:
# Better than Google

*All the answers are inside your family.*

▷ With over 1.1 million followers on TikTok (or 'Soul Tok', as he calls it), Michael Armstrong is one of the leading 'messengers' in the past life space. Ever since he had his own spiritual awakening in 2007, he has been gathering and distilling complex information about past lives and trying to package it in a way that interests and excites people. And he's certainly achieved that with his series, *Reality-Bending Things Kids Say*.

When I interviewed Michael, his online series included 13 videos with over 20 million views and hundreds of thousands of comments. It all began when he shared a famous past life case with his community—the story of a three-year-old boy in Syria who appeared to remember where he'd been murdered.[1] After Michael shared this case on his TikTok account, it opened the floodgates. He was inundated with messages from parents whose children had seemingly mystical revelations.

*'When my daughter was two, I heard her talking to someone. I asked her who and she said, "Your daddy, Tony." My dad died four years*

*before she was born. I'd also never mentioned him or his name to her, ever.'*

*'When my daughter was three, she kissed my tummy and said, "Bye." When I asked why, she said, "My sister had to go but she'd be back." I had a miscarriage the next day.'*

*'My son recently told me, "Mummy, did you know our souls were friends before I lived in your belly. I couldn't wait to see you again." He is six.'*

*'At the age of four, my daughter walked up to me out of the blue and said, "I was dead under the water for two years." And then just walked away.'*

*'When my son was five, I told him he had beautiful eyes. He said, "Thank you, my grandma picked them out." His grandma died 10 days before he was born.'*

*'My son said he was an old man. He went to sleep and woke up with me as his mum.'*

*'My three-year-old daughter saw a pic of my dad who passed away a year before she was born and said, "I'm sorry I had to go mummy." I bawled and still do thinking of it.'*[2]

The stories that Michael shares range from cute to heart-warming and even, at times, disturbing. One little girl told her mum, 'Mummy, I'm really glad I chose you to be my mummy this time. My other mummy, before you, killed me.' Someone commented underneath the video, 'Pro: low standard. Just make sure to keep her alive and she'll be impressed. #toosoon #notfunny.'

Most of the parents who reach out to him are confused, says Michael. This isn't the kind of parenting query that you can simply ask Google. Unsurprisingly, parents don't know how to react, and their instinct is often to ignore or dismiss their kid's comments. Michael is sympathetic. It has been over a decade since he had his own *satori* moment—a Buddhist term for a sudden, flash of enlightenment—whilst standing in his kitchen. At the time he was a Christian and was in a heated conversation with a friend, who was an atheist. The topic? Artificial intelligence and life and death. If you created a robot with enough artificial intelligence, it would seem consciously aware. When you unplugged it, there would be nothingness ... no heaven for the robot.

'In my mind, at the time, something clicked,' says Michael. 'I felt a sense of fear. The systems which I've built my beliefs upon crumbled.' And then something happened ... As he tells it, a tunnel of light opened in front of him. 'I zoomed through this tunnel of light,' says Michael. 'I saw this ball of light— like a sun—with water droplets of light bouncing off it.' During this experience, he received a message:

*'All these droplets of light are souls having a unique experience and then splashing back into the source of everything. Death is not the end; it continues on and on.'*

Michael believes he'd be more sceptical if it wasn't for his mate, the atheist. When he 'came back' into his kitchen, his friend had a strange look on his face. At the same time, they'd had exactly the same experience. Today, Michael no longer identifies as a Christian, but has spent sending over a decade researching every major religion and philosophy. 'Now, I don't consider myself one religion,' he adds. 'My religion is love. There is a mass awakening happening on this planet. People are looking for answers.'

## ▷ All the Answers We're Seeking

If you're a parent, I'm sure you'll agree that we're always looking for answers to something. Why does my kid have a stomach ache? What's this weird rash? When will my toddler sleep through the night? What's the name of the blue dog from Paw Patrol?

According to one study, a curious child asks 73 questions a day (is that all?) and parents don't know the answer to half of them.[3] So, we spend our lives on Google, quizzing our mother's group or living in Facebook forums. If that doesn't work, we lay awake at night hoping the answer will fall out of the ceiling.

We condemn our kids for asking so many damn questions but, as adults, we're just as desperate for answers to life's mysteries and our own inner puzzles. To me, one of the first steps in past life parenting is really starting to listen to our children; not only the questions they ask but the answers they appear to come out with from nowhere.

I'm going to drop a little truth bomb here: it's possible that your child has already told you about a past life and you just didn't notice. Hey, it's happened to me. Because, let's be honest, our kids say a lot of stuff. And they seem to remember ... everything!

They also have no concept of time (or they realise that, actually, time isn't linear, which is a topic that we have ahead of us). To my kids, everything happened 'last week'. They were sick last week. We went on holiday last week. In our household, the sentence 'remember last week, when ...' can be followed by anything that happened during their lifetime (or, perhaps even a previous lifetime). But have you paid attention to the categories and commonalities they seem to remember? What themes are they locking into their core memory; what seems to matter most to them; what do they really want to talk about?

If your child is of school age and writes a journal as part of their classwork, it can be very revealing. In an old journal, my six-year-old wrote about how she's 'grateful for her family' but wishes 'mummy wouldn't be so cranky.' Ouch! She also came home with an illustrated picture book that she'd created, titled, *Up to the Stars*. It describes how, after we die, we become a star and then we can choose whether to come back to earth. My favourite line that she wrote is: 'Everybody dies ... and that's okay! You have a big life.'

It reminds me of a mum I interviewed for this book, whose 10-year-old girl recalled a dream in which she appeared to die and be reborn again. She told her mum:

*'Mum, I had this dream the other night, but it wasn't a dream. I was in Egypt and the pyramids were half-built. It was like this portal appeared in front of me. I could see my soul, which looked like a flame with a core in the centre. There was another flame with a core—I knew it was your soul. And we collided. That's when my soul came into my now-body.'*[4]

There is a reason I'm kicking off this book with the simple premise of 'just' listening to our kids, because it can feel like one of the hardest challenges of parenthood. We're multi-tasking; we're exhausted; we have multiple children to juggle. But past life parenting is really only, at its core, about listening. It's about listening when our kids tell us about a dream; when they have a fear that feels silly to us; when they recognise a face or place that should be new to them; when they point out a truth that we've been avoiding.

It can be uncomfortable and inconvenient, but it's worth it. Because, when a child (or an adult) remembers a past life or taps into their inner wisdom, it can act as a cheat-sheet for your entire family. We get a glimpse under a veil to the person they used to be, and a clearer picture of our own journey. As Michael experienced with his *satori* moment, we can even get a glimpse of the meaning of life. That's why past life parenting is about learning to value the breadcrumbs our children are dropping (not the crumbs in their car seat; the ones that can lead us to a deeper truth and understanding). The problem is: are we too busy parenting to notice them?

## ▷ Are We Forced to Forget?

Why have I talked about listening to your children so early in this book? Because, to me, it's the first step, and there's no time like the present. When it comes to past life memories in particular, the window isn't open forever. The average age of a child when they start to remember a past life memory is 35 months (that's about three years old), according to The University of Virginia. As children develop their verbal skills, they can come out with more detailed descriptions. Usually, by school age they stop talking about their past life memories.[5]

The question is: do they remember less, or have they learnt to hide their memories for fear of being frowned upon? It's likely to be a bit of both. We all have a degree of 'infantile amnesia'— our tendency to forget memories which happen before the age of seven. Then there's our inbuilt tendency to not want to be 'other'. Psychologists typically agree that there are five levels of self-awareness in childhood development. At level four (around the age of four, although it can be earlier), our old friend self-consciousness hits like a brick. Children are not only aware of what they are, but how they look in the eyes of others.[6]

You could say, this is a good thing: do you really want your kid wandering around sharing their inner wisdom and trusting their intuition to the exclusivity of anything else? Of course not! That could create a generation who actually trust their inner compass, challenge the status quo and could raise the earth's vibration! Sounds terrible, huh? The problem is that we're all fearful. Fear is a common emotion for most parents, especially mothers. We're scared of messing them up; of praising too much; of listening too little; of crushing their self-esteem or risking creating little emperors. Are we so concerned with getting it 'right', that we overlook our most powerful resource: our deep, inner wisdom?

David Stevens is one of Australia's most highly-rated mediums who has predicted major events long before they happened, including COVID-19, Donald Trump's presidency and the war in the Ukraine. He also does one-on-one readings with clients but be warned, they book out quickly! David says that children up until the age of six or seven are 'earth's real spiritual leaders', who can read auras, communicate with spirits and remember past lives. In his words, 'This is before the ego and social conditioning takes hold'. Imagine a world where we nurtured our kid's natural abilities.

Although David 'talks to dead people', he does believe in past lives too (we'll explain this in a later chapter). Looking back on his childhood, David can't remember connecting to spirit. He does, however, remember having a strong gut feeling. 'It's crucially important for parents that, when you do have children who have extra-sensory abilities, to encourage it,' he says. 'Ask them questions. Make them feel safe and secure. We can't look at children with our own eyes and expect them to see the world we see'.[7]

Here's the twist: it might not all be true! Research has found, children learn to lie effectively between the ages of two and four. In fact, it's an important part of their development—a milestone moment, when they realise that their minds are separate to their parents. But that doesn't mean that we should dismiss what they say, just because it doesn't fit within our belief system. Research shows[8] that one of the leading reasons that children lie is to protect someone else's feelings. If they are telling you something which seems unusual or controversial, they are going against their innate desire to fit in. To me, that means it's worth listening to.

I'll say it again: it's not easy to always be listening! This morning, my five-year-old son gave me a detailed description of every Marvel superhero character, whilst my three-year-old gabbled about Playdough and my six-year-old told me an elaborate dream about a unicorn. So, how can we really tune into our kids, whilst still having time to go to the toilet alone?

This is where our own inner knowing as parents comes into play. On some level, do you intuitively know when your child is trying to tell you something important? The air shifts, you feel guilty for being distracted; maybe a voice in your head, which is driven by fear, tells you not to believe them. As a rule of thumb, if I don't want to talk about a topic with my kids, it's probably a sign that I need to. This could mean talking to our kids about death, chatting to them about a nightmare that triggers your own insecurities, or just validating their own gut feelings, even if it makes you uncomfortable.

'As parents, we want to guide and protect our children,' adds David. 'But it's about allowing them to flourish within their own understanding. Especially for children who may reference seeing children at the end of their bed or connecting with grandparents who have crossed over; there are reasons—valid reasons—why those spirits are connecting with those children.'

This isn't about probing your kids for answers. The University of Virginia recommends asking open-ended questions and empathising with a child's feelings, but not becoming so focused on the statements that they lose sight of the fact that the current life is most important[9]. Most parents know that you don't need to probe—our kids come out with mic-drop moments when you least expect it. My little boy is full of fart jokes and stories about ninjas but, if I can keep at least one ear open, I don't miss his random revelations. This morning, over cornflakes, he told me: 'Mummy, when I squint my eyes, I can see sparkles like it's another world. Sometimes, I even see people in front of me.' Our kids come out with these announcements so lightly, and move on so quickly, that it's easy to miss them. But it's one of the magical parts of childhood, which makes the tough days endurable—the reminders that our children are sent partly to inspire and expand us.

And if your kids are over school age, don't worry, it's not too late. David didn't discover his clairvoyant gifts until he was in his mid-twenties. 'During my childhood, I don't remember connecting with spirits,' he says. 'For me, I always had a strong gut feeling.' It was another medium who pointed out that maybe he had a deeper knowing. 'I was an open-minded sceptic, but I had a childlike curiosity about it,' says David. 'We can learn that childlike curiosity from our children too. I wanted to grow more, to learn more and feel more—and that's what kids are doing with general life.'

## Chapter 2 ▷ Thinking Points

▷ Can you think of a time when you listened to Google or another non-expert, instead of your own inner wisdom—how did it work out for you?

▷ Are there any common themes or patterns in the memories your kids come out with?

▷ How would it feel to choose to believe your children?

▷ Have you ever experienced a moment when your child has come out with a mic-drop statement, which delivered a surprise solution?

▷ How could you approach parenting with more childlike curiosity, openness, and trust in yourself?

# Chapter 3:
# **Triggers & Glimmers**

*The greatest antidote to fear is feeling seen.*

▷  A lot of the past life memories that kids come up with can be filed in the cute category, but some are more sinister. When he was three years old, Angela's* son began talking about such strange events that she began to take notes on her phone. When I put a call-out on my Instagram asking for anecdotes of kids with past life memories, Angela sent her notes to me. His recollections proved to be pretty surprising, even shocking.

At first, he talked about his parents who lived in Africa. (In this life, he was born and raised in Australia.) He said that he lived in a house with a chimney that 'you can't get in.' He called it a 'safe house' and remembered their family living there during the winter. He didn't have any siblings, he said, but would talk about two adults, Shaun and Johnny. At the age of four, he explained to his mum, 'One day, Jonny smashed his phone. That was a bad day. That was the day I came into your tummy.'[1]

Like many children who remember past lives, he was very matter of fact and came out with these memories when his mum least expected it. One day, when she was putting bubble bath in the tub, he said, 'I never saw this from my other parents, they never put these many bubbles in.' Now, at the age of six, he no longer talks about those memories.

This is the side of past life recollection that we don't like to consider as a parent and yet it's not uncommon. According to Jim Tucker and his team at The University of Virginia, many kids seem to remember troubling memories about past lives, including how they died and even who killed them. 'We have done psychological testing with some of the children,' said Dr. Tucker in an interview for the Mind, Body, Green podcast. 'They don't show any psychiatric disturbance. The only thing that comes out is, they tend to be very bright and very verbal.'[2]

Research suggests a very clear link between past life memories and present-day fears and phobias. A study from the University of Virginia, led by Doctor Tucker's predecessor, Doctor Ian Stevenson, found that, in children who remembered dying of 'unnatural' means, 35 per cent of those children showed an unnatural fear towards the way they died.[3] Here are two examples from Doctor Stevenson's study:

▷ One child remembered a life as a man who had gorged himself on yogurt that had been contaminated and then died of severe gastroenteritis. In this life, he showed a marked aversion for yogurt.
▷ Another example occurred in a child who remembered the life of a young woman who died after a prolonged illness due to congenital heart disease; the child had a severe phobia of drugs, injections, and blood.

The phobias usually manifested between the ages of two and five. Sometimes, the child began to show the phobia in early infancy and only recalled the relatable past life memory later. The fear didn't seem to be caused by another incident and their family members didn't share the phobia. As Doctor Stevenson wrote, 'They seem to require some paranormal explanation—of which, reincarnation is only one possible option.' Throughout Doctor Stevenson's career, he always avoided the word proof and presented his cases with open-minded curiosity.

As a parent, it might feel like a scary prospect. (What parent wants their child to remember being chased or murdered?) But it could also provide a missing piece to a puzzle. Why is your child so scared of water? Why do they scream during every car trip? Why are they so scared of the dark in a way they're not growing out of. Why do they struggle so much with separation anxiety? Of course, a lot of these issues can be put down to 'normal' childhood development. But could there be another explanation—and could it help us, as parents, to better support our children when they're struggling?

In my research, I spoke to a number of parents who had linked a chronic fear, which their child experienced, to a potential past life memory. One little boy would only sit in the passenger side of any car. He would scream blue murder if they tried to put him in the car seat behind the driver's seat. When playing with his Lego cars one day, he told his mum: '[The Lego man] can't go in that seat. That's where I was sitting when our car crashed.' He had never been in a car crash in this life. And, yes, he would only seat his Lego man on the passenger side of his toy vehicle. He was adamant.

This is where past life parenting can give us a shot of patience— even if it doesn't solve the situation. When our child has a chronic fear of a certain situation or sensation, it can feel debilitating for a parent to deal with, and leave us feeling at the end of our tether. It can also cause serious 'compassion fatigue'. We start off patient and loving, then transition to annoyed and frustrated. And throw in a dose of embarrassment if other people witness it. It can also be easy to belittle it ('you're fine, it's just water'). One gift of past life parenting is it increases our compassion quota. Even if your child hasn't mentioned a past life memory in which they drowned, you can start to wonder what's possible ... could they? Remember how we mentioned that curiosity is the antidote of anxiety. That brief moment of wondering 'is there something else behind it' can give you the space to breathe again.

## ▷ Lightning Strikes & Loud Noises

Eli Bliliuos is a certified hypnotist based in New York City who specialises in past life regressions. He has worked with adults and children on phobias and fears relating to past life memories. One of his most memorable clients was a reporter who had a very conservative background. She came to him for clinical hypnotherapy relating to a phobia. During the session she had a 'spontaneous past life regression'—where she remembered a past life without being coaxed.

'As she was leaving, she said, "Well, I don't believe in anything I just experienced. I think it's all in my imagination,"' recalls Eli. 'She called me back four weeks later and said, "I still don't believe what happened was a past life, but my phobia has gone."' To Eli that is the most important thing: that it works. 'I told her to look at it like a metaphor,' he adds. 'You don't have to believe it, but I'm glad it helped you.'[4]

He had another client who had a crippling fear of lightning. During a past life regression, they remembered dying in a battle. 'As they were dying, there was lightning in the background,' adds Eli. 'That leads to a fear of thunder and lightning. After our session, that fear no longer existed. It's about re-experiencing it, reframing it and then moving forward.'

The same could be true of a child who hates loud noises. In a former life, were they a soldier on a battlefield? If your child has a fear of abandonment or separation, did they lose a parent, sibling or their own child in a past life? And then there's the (huge) topic of female suppression and the way that girls and women who were seen as witches were treated. We'll go into this in the chapter on *Tweens, Teens & Transitions.* (So, buckle up, it's a good one!).

If your child has an illogical phobia, Eli does suggest exploring past life regression. This is different to the advice of The University Virginia who recommend against putting a child through past life regression hypnosis. It's worth reiterating that Doctor Tucker and his team rely on 'spontaneous statements' made by children about their past lives to provide clues and insights.[5] The University of Virginia recommends that parents chat to their kids about past life memories, but also focus on the present. Their website advises: 'It might be helpful to explain that while they may have had another family in a previous life, their current family is the one they have for this life ... Parents should acknowledge and value what their children have told them while making clear that the past life is truly in the past.'[6]

Personally, I'm a fan of spontaneous past life recollection—when you appear to recall a past life during a guided meditation or another type of spiritual healing such as reiki, or even during a dream. Despite writing a book on past life parenting, I haven't sent any of my children to a past life regressionist and I don't plan to. (They can always explore that when they're older.) But, since discovering past life parenting, I do look at their fears and phobias through a new lens. Could they be deeper than the fear that's in front of us? And how can we begin to explore their triggers and glimmers, and piece together the puzzle of their phobias to, hopefully, complete their trauma cycle?

## ▷ Dealing with Panic Stations

When it comes to fears and phobia, Eli encourages parents to trust their gut feeling. 'I always believe there is a part of us that intuitively knows [if a fear is from a past life],' he says. 'I spend a good deal of my time, when I work with clients, telling them to trust what comes to them. Trust now and analyse it later. The intuitive part of you knows exactly what you need.'

To me, you don't have to pinpoint the exact past life moment that created a trigger. I don't think it always helps to play detective. But there is something grounding about choosing to see that your child's fear is very real to them, even if it seems illogical to you in the moment. I've spoken to parents who believe their daughter's fear of going to the doctors is linked to a past life where she lived through the plague in the UK. (When the COVID-19 pandemic hit, she kept talking about the 'last time' this happened to her in England.)

I spoke to a dad who can't grow a beard because his son says it reminds him of his 'old dad' and it makes him miss him. These kids are passionate and adamant about their likes, dislikes and recollections.

This isn't about mollycoddling or always giving into your child's desires (wait for our chapter on *Autonomy & Freedom*). But, once you begin joining the dots, it can really take you anywhere. So, how can you begin to explore it? When your own child has an intense, recurring fear or a phobia, pause and think:

▷ What is your own parental intuition trying to tell you?

▷ Does this feel deeper than a 'normal' fear?

▷ Are they acting as if they're in very dire danger?

A game-changer for me has been the advice of clinical psychologist, Doctor Becky Kennedy, the author of the book *Good*

*Inside* and the creator of the community of the same name. Her work focuses on the 'parent behind the parenting' and the 'child behind the behaviour' with the powerful premise: every child is good inside. I should make it clear; her research is not related to reincarnation or to any kind of spiritual topic, but I think that it's relevant anyway. According to Dr. Becky, the three most important words we can say to our children are this:

*'I believe you.'*

I believe that you believe what you're feeling. I believe that your reaction is very real to you. 'This is the language that parents need in the in-between,' says Dr. Becky. These are the moments when we want to hold a decision that feels right as a parent, and still see, name, and validate a kid's experience as real. She gives these examples[7]:

*'I believe the water is cold. We paid for this [swimming] lesson. I really believe you can finish it and then we can reassess lessons going forward.'*

*'I believe it's really hard to be in a toy store and not buy something for yourself. I believe you want this one so badly. I'm going to take a picture of it. My answer is still no. I believe this is so hard for you. I'm going to hold you as we're leaving the store.'*

So, how does this relate to the pillars of past life parenting, and common fears and phobias? To me, it's all about validating our kid's emotions and reactions, even when they're inconvenient to us. It's also about removing the judgement of all feelings (positive and negative) to see them as a simple self-protection mechanism that always comes from somewhere.

Our fearless children can feel like our favourite children, because they make it easier for your family to function. However, I've also found that my fearful children are my most rewarding children because when I get it 'right', and I feel like I've supported them well, I feel like a rockstar. For your family, this could look sound something like this:

*'I believe you're feeling very fearful right now.'*

*'I believe you don't like the energy in this place.'*

*'I believe your dream felt very real.'*

*'I believe you and I'm here to support you. We will work this out together.'*

Here's the good bit: you don't have to find an instant solution. Oh, what a relief that is! This isn't something you have to fix right now. You can remind yourself, this isn't an emergency. (I used to have that phrase stuck in my kitchen for the chaos of mornings.) Your kid might feel under threat when there's a lawn mower buzzing outside, but you know they're not. Every time they have a big reaction, you don't have to react with the energy of an ambulance siren.

As a side note, it's also a powerful opportunity to explore your own fears and phobias, especially the ones you feel embarrassed and ashamed about. If we're going to extend this much empathy and compassion to our children, we should also extend the same love and understanding to ourselves. The next time that you feel triggered by a space, face or place, try telling yourself: 'I believe you and I'm here to support you. We'll figure this out together.'

Telling our children we believe them isn't encouraging them to double-down on their fears. It's actually the first step to easing their triggers by showing them we're fully present, and won't turn away from them.

### Glimmers: The Good Stuff

As we're talking about triggers, I want to lighten the mood by talking about the other end of the spectrum: glimmers. Glimmers are like the opposite of triggers—small moments that spark joy or peace, that can help cue our nervous system to feel safe or calm. It could be a sound, a sight, a smell, a person or an activity that makes you feel like you are 'home'.

You probably see your child experience a glimmer every week, or even every day, especially when they're babies and toddlers. The moment when they see your face at day care pick-up. When your baby winds their fingers in the back of your hair. When you're sitting in a bubble bath together. Glimmer, glimmer, glimmer away!

This is the great news, I'm here to share. When we begin to explore past life parenting, we don't only understand what makes our kids fearful but also what makes them happy—and, to me, that's always a victory! According to Doctor Stevenson's work[8], many kids with past life memories 'play-act' their old occupation, whether they were a baker, a doctor or even a chimney sweep. It appears that a job or career that made them feel fulfilled in the past can create an imprint and rub off on their present life behaviour.

How can this play out in your family? Well, you don't have to do anything excessive. It could look like gently encouraging your kid's natural interests: the costume they want to wear; the random hobby they want to explore; the way they want to wear their hair; the outfit that doesn't seem at all appropriate. What makes them feel happy, connected and valued?

Whilst researching this book, I heard from one dad whose son suddenly said he wanted to go fishing. (It was not something their family had ever discussed.) When his dad asked why his son wanted to go fishing, the boy replied, 'Because I used to go fishing with my other dad and family—not in this time but in a time before this time.' So, the family went fishing and it ended up leading to a great bonding opportunity. The little boy loved it as much as he knew he would on a soul-level.

There's another upside to tapping into our kid's past life glimmers—it can add variety and spontaneity to our lives. Research shows, embracing variety in life makes us happier and more content, but we can all be creatures of habit. Our kids tend to gravitate towards the hobbies that we nudge them in; the things we liked to do in our own childhood. Well, your weekends could be a lot more diverse, and therefore satisfying, if they embrace a different hobby from a past life, which their 'old' family loved to do together.

When I was researching this book, I put a call-out on a media platform for people whose children have appeared to remember past life memories. One of the many people who contacted me was leadership expert, Juliet Robertson—and I instantly fell in love with her story. Juliet specialises in helping people to develop self-awareness and communication skills in order to grow trust—a skillset which came in handy when her daughter, now sixteen, began recalling a past life experience.

'She was five or six-years-old when it first began,' says Juliet. 'She said to me, "I used to be a maid in a big house in the country in the Victorian era." She remembered her uniform. She was adamant, she needed to go to school in England.' There was a family connection to the UK—they had relatives living there, but they weren't in touch with them.

Over the next few years, her daughter's attachment to Victorian England continued. At school, every Book Week, she'd dress up as Victorian characters. One year she walked around with a set of big, old-fashioned keys tied around her waist as if she was running a big household. 'She was interested in that period in history,' says Juliet. 'She would set up a tuberculosis hospital with her little friends in her room. I remember her going to stay with a school friend when she was seven, and she offered to clean their house. She just said, "This is who I am."'

As a leadership coach, Juliet teaches the importance of 'soft skills'—skills that help you to work harmoniously with people. So, how did she respond to her daughter? 'With her love of England, we didn't dismiss it at all,' says Juliet. 'I was very much: tell me about it.'

But there were limits. The family were not going to move to England just so their daughter could go to school there. So, they came up with a compromise: you can go when you're older. As their daughter progressed through school, she talked about it less and then not at all; however, a tie to England remains. When I interviewed Juliet, the family had just returned from a two-week holiday in the UK and there was talk of her daughter doing summer study at Cambridge. 'She says she doesn't want to live in London,' says Juliet. 'But she could easily live in the country in England— that's what she enjoys. There's definitely still a link there.'

It reminds me of the 'Circle of Security' parenting program. Based on 50-years of early childhood development, the program aims to create a 'secure attachment' between parents and their children. Imagine holding your hands in a cup shape—this is your child's 'secure base' and 'safe haven'. When a child leaves the secure base to explore the world, they need parents to 'watch over me, help me, delight in me, enjoy me.' When it's time for the child to come back to their safe haven, they need parents to 'protect me, comfort, me, delight in me, organise my feelings.'[9]

Is this our role in supporting these children who seem to remember past life memories? How can we create such a safe haven from which they can explore their soul memories, identify their soul purpose and still comfort them when it's necessary?

It isn't always easy. Indeed, paying attention to our kid's fears and phobias can feel far easier and more natural than tuning into what brings them pleasure. It's a survival mechanism to be alert to the threats to our family. It can feel frivolous to focus our attention on their elaborate desires ... but it's also crucial. The world needs more fun, pleasure and playfulness. It doesn't just nurture our kids; it makes parenting a whole lot more enjoyable.

In my own family, I can see evidence of past life glimmers. I was still pregnant with my daughter when I learnt, during my own past life healing, that she had been a pagan herbalist in her past life. That's when I was shown the image of her walking through fog-covered fields, gathering nuts and berries for herbal medicines. I was told she'd have a strong bond with my husband, her dad, because of their shared love of nature. (He is an environmental scientist)

This didn't change how I parented her, as we have always been an outdoorsy family, but it has made me more observant of the situations that make her sparkle. I watch her as she skips down a forest path wearing a tutu, filling her pockets with leaves and nuts, with a smile on my face. I always try to say yes when she wants to join my husband in the garden. We talk about fairies, gnomes and the spirits that live in the trees.

I put as much effort into showing interest in her past life hobbies, as I do in the passions she has picked-up in this life. To me, it's an investment in her past and an investment in her future, because I want her to grow-up to be a woman who values joy and pleasure. I can't tell you whether the past life I was shown is correct, but I can tell you how it feels to acknowledge what makes her happy. It feels warm, comforting, spacious and light. In a world filled with fear, it feels like a remedy.

## Chapter 3 ▷ Thinking Points

▷ Can you think of an intense fear that you or your child experience, which feels deeper than a 'normal' aversion?

▷ Could it give you more patience or acceptance to consider that this fear might be caused by a past life experience?

▷ This week, can you practise using those three important words in your parenting: I believe you.

▷ Notice if you're more aware of your child's triggers than your glimmers, and how you can make more space to nurture pleasure.

▷ Know that there is no rush to fix anything. This is not an emergency. Breathe.

# Chapter 4:
# **Autonomy & Personal Freedom**

*Our children's job is to place us outside our comfort zone.*

▷ Rebecca Maklad and her husband had left their daughter, Tigerlily, with her grandmother whilst they went out for dinner when the little girl first started talking about her 'other life' in Egypt. Her dad's side of the family is Egyptian so, on some level, it didn't seem unusual—until she began talking about her other family in more detail. 'When we called to check on her, Sophie [her grandmother] said, "Tigerlily has just woken from her dream with a detailed story about her other life in Egypt,"' recalls Rebecca. 'She said she was Tutankhamun's daughter and that Isis was her mum'.[1] If you're not up to scratch on your Egyptian theology, Isis is the goddess of healing and magic.

Most parents would assume that it was just a dream but, over the next few years, Tigerlily's attraction to Ancient Egypt only grew stronger. 'A sceptic could say, she's just from an Egyptian family,' adds Rebecca. 'But, she is obsessed with Ancient Egypt documentaries. At the age of four, she will watch full, adult documentaries every single night before bed. She can tell you the details of every Egyptian god and goddess. She can take you through the mummification process in detail.' The week of our interview,

Tigerlily was watching the documentary *Tutankhamun's Daughters* on repeat. When Tutankhamun's tomb was uncovered, it contained the mummified bodies of two small babies—blood tests suggest that they are likely to be his twin children[2].

As parents go, Rebecca is naturally open. With a background in events and branding, she is the founder of Soulful Influence, which helps individuals and organisations to tap into their purpose and create a brand which aligns with their soul mission. Despite her acceptance of all things spiritual, she recognises that she is also a parent and, as such, must set boundaries. 'When Tigerlily started school, I had to say to her, "Maybe just talk about Ancient Egypt life at home with mummy,"' adds Rebecca. 'It was a hard one, as I didn't want to shut it down. I want to nurture her intuition, and this aspect of her. But, at the same time, how do you protect her energy in that environment at school? She didn't ask why. She just said okay. It was very matter of fact for her.'

When it comes to past life memories and kids who seem very intuitive, the topic of personal autonomy and personal freedom is a big one. How do we encourage our kid's inner knowing, whilst setting healthy boundaries and limits? When do we support them; when do we indulge them; and how far do we let them follow their inner compass?

As Rebecca has learnt, it's on a case-per-case basis. It comes back to our old friend: trusting your intuition. Two days prior to our interview, when Rebecca dropped Tigerlily at school, she discovered that her usual teacher wouldn't be there today. 'Tigerlily completely lost it,' says Rebecca. 'I went to go and get the [replacement] teacher she was going to have but Tigerlily wouldn't have a bar of it. Eventually we had to take her outside and her principal came out to talk to us.'

AUTONOMY & PERSONAL FREEDOM

The beauty of this moment was that it gave them time to pause. There was no rush to solve the problem or gloss over the issue. Eventually, the Principal suggested that Tigerlily join a different class with a different teacher—and she skipped off into school happily. Later, Rebecca reflected on the experience: 'When I tuned into that first [replacement] teacher, I didn't dig her energy either,' she says. 'She seemed abrasive. I would have felt overwhelmed and anxious too, just like Tigerlily, if I had felt forced to go to her.'

Of course, it's not always possible to let our kids get their own way, even if they're tapping into a deeper intuition. But, for these kids, the adage that 'a parent is always right' isn't going to cut it. 'For me, it's about finding a balance,' says Rebecca. 'And it's about giving them language to express themselves. It's about acknowledging that a lot of kids in the playground is overwhelming, energetically. Helping her to understand that she is an empath and how can I arm her effectively?'

One of the main messages of this book is: our children are way wiser than we give them credit for. But, on an anatomical level, you can't ignore their limitations. Our brains are not fully formed until our mid to late twenties. The part of the brain that controls impulses, the prefrontal cortex, is one of the final parts to mature.

Anyone who has watched a toddler in a supermarket, screaming because they can't have a lollypop, knows that their lack of impulse control is very real. So, it's not just a case of trusting their instincts. There must be an element of parental intervention, for their sake and for our own wellbeing.

## ▷ Your Child is a Whole Soul

Ashley Hämäläinen is an Akashic Record Reader and the founder of A Line Within. In case you're not familiar with the Akashic Records, I'll explain it as simply as possible. The idea is, we can also access an 'energetic library' of everything we've lived, experienced and thought in this life and previous lives. If we can access these records, they can give us incredible clarity.

After the birth of my third baby, I completed my training in how to 'access' the Akashic Records with Ashley. I don't enter them often, but I will go 'there' when I'm stuck on a decision or at a crossroads. (The title of this book came after an Akashic Record Reading with myself.)

Ashley is a great example of a metaphysical parent who allows her children a lot of autonomy. A mum of two, she has supported her young daughter to change her first name twice. (It's currently Honu). In an Instagram post, she explained her reasoning. 'When she was one-and-a-half, she renamed herself,' explained Ashley. 'Then, recently, she did it again. She flows through life without restriction and allows herself to fully express herself, however she feels in that moment.'[3]

Yoga teacher and feminine embodiment coach, Sarah-Jane Perman, creator of the Rewild the Mother program, is another advocate for trusting your kid's inner knowing. When her son, Sammy, started school and struggled with the transition, she would sit outside in her car for the entire day (in the hot Ibiza sun) because she promised she'd stay close to him. Once again, she shared her experience on Instagram, writing: 'My role as a mother is listening in to my innate wisdom and my child's. To mother in a way that feels natural for us is almost a revolutionary act.'[4]

For some parents, this might sound excessive and even indulgent. I might have said that too, before I gave birth to a child who has very clear personal boundaries. It comes down to circumstance: there is a time and a place for autonomy. If my son is having a 'moment' outside a toy shop because he wants to go in, I'm going to 'hold my no'. But, if he doesn't want to kiss a relative goodbye, I'm never going to make him.

So, how can we know when to cede and when to push back? Sadly, there isn't a simple answer. It comes down to seeing your child as a whole person, rather than a fragment of an adult who doesn't deserve autonomy until a double-digit milestone in the future.

It reminds me of the work of parenting coach Janet Lansbury whose podcast, *Unruffled* is a must-listen for parents. She urges parents to see their child as a 'whole person', even when they're infants.[5] Her parenting principles include 'hear me, don't just fix me' and 'trusting them with your truth'. Sound familiar? As a parenting expert, Janet does make it clear: we shouldn't treat infants as small grownups. 'They need a baby's life,' she writes. 'But, they deserve the same level of human respect that we give to adults.'

At the moment, I have a motherhood affirmation on my fridge that reads, 'My children respect each other, because I respect and love them.' Yes, I wrote it after a conflict-filled school holidays, but it's also an important reminder. The old way of parenting was based on fear and conforming, and it created fearful, conforming adults. If we want our children to be love, they have to know love. If we want our children to be respectful, they need to feel respected.

Giving our kids more autonomy can feel scary, but it can also be a chance to exhale as a family. We don't have to feel like a prison warden in our own home. Like most parenting lessons, it comes down to balance. If I let my kids fully self-govern themselves, they'd order pizza every day and fall asleep on the floor from exhaustion. We can listen to, and value, their desires and self-expressions, whilst 'holding our no' when we think it's appropriate.

This is where the naysayers will argue that 'children don't know what's best for them.' Well, this brings us to the other half of the autonomy equation ... If we want children to make decisions in their best interest, we need to teach children to read their own inner compass; their intuition. So, how do we do that? I'm going to unpack it ...

## ▷ Raising Kids Who Trust Their Instincts

Dana Childs is an intuitive, an energy healer and a medium. For seven years, she also worked as a teacher before discovering her gifts in clairvoyance. She says that every person is born with intuitive abilities, which basically means we have a 'deeper knowing' of something. The problem is, we're often conditioned to doubt ourselves from childhood. 'How many mediums have been shut down at eight-years-old as they're told it's imaginary?' says Dana. 'All the things we want are locked up in these little souls coming through. When we can get curious about what the soul is, and suspend our own beliefs for a moment, that's how we're going to get things like the cure for cancer.'[6]

In past life parenting, the goal is to help children to trust their intuition, rather than shutting it down or doubting it. This isn't just about finding answers to everyday problems, like why your kid has a tummy ache or a fear of putting their head under water. It's also about the long game. Intuitive children grow into intuitive adults who may come up with solutions to the world's biggest problems, change global systems or work within governments. Or, they could just be exceedingly happy because they trust their inner compass and don't have to chase constant validation. Doesn't that sound blissful?

Whether your child seems to remember a past life memory or has an instinctive feeling that doesn't align with you, Dana recommends a three-pronged approach for parents:
  ▷ *Be curious*
  ▷ *Listen*
  ▷ *Allow your children to explore, within reason.*

One mother came to Dana for guidance when her son, who was six years old at the time, reported seeing deceased relatives in his bedroom. He also told his mum, he'd once been a firefighter and that he'd died in a 'tall building fire'. Now, he was terrified of going into tall buildings.

His mother, who was raised as a Christian, was struggling to get her head around it all. To help the family, Dana offered this advice: 'Start asking questions and get curious about what he's seeing. Our kids learn how to name shapes and know a dog goes 'woof' because we reinforce it. So, normalise what is unseen for you but experienced for him.'

By asking questions, the mum gathered more information. She was able to match the name that her son gave to a firefighter who was killed in 9/11. By gently exploring her son's memories, they worked through his fear of tall buildings. Most importantly, it was a special bonding experience for mother and son.

'It became one of the most beautiful family awakenings,' says Dana. 'That family showed me what power lies when we're able to take our kids as they are. We're not telling them they're wrong. We can get curious and normalise their experience.'

Another important step in nurturing intuition is to stop hiding your own feelings as a caregiver. Every time your child sees that you're sad and you say, 'No, no, mummy is fine', it's having the opposite effect on them. 'When you say, "no, no, mummy is happy", are you really?' asks Dana. 'Because, in that moment, you have damaged your child's intuition.'

That doesn't mean you have to share all the nitty-gritty details of your inner conflict, but you can own your feelings in an age-appropriate manner, whilst ensuring that your child doesn't feel like it's their responsibility to fix it. Dana recommends this strategy:

*'Are you sad, mummy?'*

*'Yes, I'm sad, but it's not your responsibility.*
*I'm going to be okay later.*
*Right now, I'm just having a feeling.'*

We often think we need to shield our children, but they are incredibly resilient, accepting and flexible when we allow them to be, especially when we haven't modelled fear and pessimism. And, sometimes, our children can even make eery predictions—and be totally chill about it.

This happened to one of Dana's clients. One morning, as their four-year-old tied his shoes, he announced, quite calmly, that his parents would get divorce in the future. At the time, his parents were shocked, as they were happily married. Years later, when that boy had become a teenager, his parents separated. At four-years-old, their son had even predicted the year it would happen.

'His mum said it was creepy at the time, but now it brings her a surprising amount of comfort,' says Dana. 'His soul knew what he was coming into. We think we'll get divorced, and it will devastate the kids. Likely, they already knew it was coming.'

## ▷ Setting Boundaries with a Reborn Child

At a very young age, our kid's intuitive feelings can be finely tuned—even science agrees with this. Research has shown that children between the age of three and eight-years-old do typically trust their own intuition over other people's knowledge. As they get older, they begin to prioritise other people's opinions, but they're still quite picky when it comes to who they listen to, (for example, a four-year-old appreciates that a mechanic knows more about cars than a doctor[7]).

Why is this good news? Well, we want our children to trust their inner compass, whilst also being open to expanding their knowledge from reputable sources. This is where Dana's three pillars come into play: be curious, listen and allow your children to explore, within reason.

So, how can we be open to seeing the unseen? It can be as simple (and complex!) as not dismissing a situation too quickly. For example:

▷ *Your child remembers a past life in which they lived on a sailing boat.* How can you explore how this memory feels in their body and try to identify any glimmers which you could recreate in your life, within your budget? This could sound like asking your child: 'Do you remember what it felt like on the boat, what you could see or the kind of places you'd go? Maybe, at the weekend, we could make boats for your teddies and see if we could sail them on the river. Or go down to the harbour for ice-cream at sunset.'

▷ *Your child says they've talked to their dead grandma.* How can you show interest in a gentle way that is free from fear or your own judgement? How can you ask questions in as neutral a way as possible? This could sound like asking your child: 'Oh, really? What do you remember grandma saying to you? Has she come to see you before? Isn't it lovely that she chose to come and remind you how much she loves you.'

▷ *They're terrified of a certain place or person.* How can you gather further details without sounding reactive or fearful, or making false promises that you'll never go to that place or see that person again. You can also encourage to be mindful and gain mastery over that emotion. This could sound like saying to your child: 'If that feeling was a colour, can you tell me what colour it would be? If that feeling was a shape, what shape would it be? Can you move it around your body? Let's get curious about it together and see if we can play with it.'

▷ *They come home with a stomach ache.* In a later chapter, we'll cover the topic of empaths and why empathic children can pick up other people's ailments or experience physical sensations around negative emotions. You can start to get curious with your child about the root cause of this feeling. This could sound like: 'D'you know, sometimes we can pick up feelings from other people by accident. Do you think this is your stomach ache or someone else's? If it's not yours, we can let it go—we don't need it anymore. Let that feeling float off into the sky.'

Some of these ideas will seem very alien at first, but you might be surprised by how open your kids are to discussing them, especially when they experience the benefits of exploring their intuition. It's also a win-win situation for the entire family. As you encourage your kids to tap into their inner compass, you can help to guide and navigate each other. I know, for a fact, that my kid's intuition can make my life better, and hold me accountable to my own boundaries. They can also act as a smoke detector for when the mood in our house shifts or it's time to take action.

When my son was less than two-years-old, he developed a persistent cough that would kick in every morning and every bedtime. It was like he was allergic to something in our house, even though I had removed all the obvious culprits. At the time, my husband and I were renting out the apartment underneath the main part of our house. We didn't realise at the time, but our tenant was … unsavoury.

Unfortunately, it took us months to be able to get rid of our tenant and the situation caused incredible stress in our household. The week we were finally able to evict our difficult tenant, my son stopped coughing—and it's never been a problem since.

I've learnt to see my son's allergies as an emotional barometer. How is the emotional environment in our home? Are my husband and I in conflict, and trying to hide it from our son? In a way, his 'itchy instincts' help us to set better boundaries in our household. I can't sweep tension under the rug, because he simply doesn't let us. (I should say, sometimes his eczema also flares up because he's eaten too much dairy; not everything is metaphysical.)

## Chapter 4 ▷ Thinking Points

▷ How can you help your kids feel seen, heard and believed, whilst also setting boundaries and standing by your decisions?

▷ When your child shares their feelings with you, how can you be curious, listen and allow them to explore within reason?

▷ How would you react differently if you gave yourself permission to pause and tune into your own intuition before making a snap judgement?

▷ Can you think of a time when your kid's instincts have made your life better? Do they give you more balance or stop you from overstepping your own boundaries? Take a moment to feel grateful for that.

# Chapter 5:
## Soul Clusters & Chosen Families

*Your children chose you and you chose them.*

From a young age, Bernadette's son would talk about his past life experiences. From as early as he could speak, he also told his mum about his 'sister, Tobi'. This was interesting because, at the time, he was an only child. In fact, Bernadette had been diagnosed with secondary infertility and was finding it difficult to conceive again. 'He was adamant, his sister was coming,' explained Bernadette, when we spoke over Instagram. 'He said, we just had to be patient.'

Five years later, against the doctor's expectations, she found out that she was pregnant again, with a little girl this time. 'When she was born, my son told me that they had been married in a past life and had chosen to come back together in this life,' says Bernadette. 'Needless to say, I bawled my eyes out.'[1]

This is just one example of many children who say that they have lived and loved family members in previous lifetimes. As this case shows, it's not always like-for-like. Your mother can become your sister. Your wife can become your brother. Your grandfather can become your best friend. It's an interesting and thought-provoking concept.

Have you ever met a person for the first time, whether it's a friend, a sexual partner or your own newborn, and felt like you'd known them for a lifetime? It's the cliché of a 'meet-cute' in a movie—that instant familiarity and connection that you can feel when you meet a special person. Well, how would you feel if I told you that this feeling may be on-point. Your first meeting might be more of a reunion.

In the spiritual space, it's called a 'soul group' or a 'soul cluster'— the group of important people who we find our way back to, lifetime after lifetime after lifetime. Like all things in the matter of reincarnation, the goal is to evolve together or to complete an agreement in our Soul Contract. There's also the small matter of eternal love—it seems that our love does transcend time and space and is strong enough to pull us back together.

In a TikTok story, Doctor Toni Reilly, a past life and reincarnation specialist who I interviewed for this book, listed 'seven signs that your child has been your mother in a past life'— and the post got a lot of interest. Here are the signs, she outlined[2]:

- ▷ **They're bossy.** This child tells you how things are.
- ▷ **They're sticky.** This child is never far from your side.
- ▷ **They're advanced.** This child is mature, even as a toddler.
- ▷ **They're domestic.** This child is confident with domestic duties.
- ▷ **They're responsible.** They check in on you throughout life.
- ▷ **They're loyal.** They'll stand up to anyone doing the wrong things by you.
- ▷ **You're friends.** As adults, you're friends and enjoy each other's company.

If your child ticks these boxes, this might start to intrigue you. Could you kid really be your former parent? What I found more interesting was the comments section of the post and the stories of other parents who had an inclination that their child was once their mother (some, because their child told them so!). Here are some of the comments left under Doctor Reilly's original post:

*'Omg! My daughter told me when she was two that it's her turn to be the baby and my turn to be the mum because she was my mum before.'*

*'I want to cry. This is exactly my daughter and myself. She's the most loyal and loving person I know. She says I am her best friend.'*

*'In the first three weeks of my daughter's life, every time I looked in her eyes, I had the overwhelming feeling she wasn't a baby, she knew way more than a baby.'*

*'My daughter told me she used to be my mum and hates that now I tell her what to do.'*

*'My daughter was about three when she looked me straight in the eye and said, "Do you remember the time when I was your mother?"'*

When it comes to rebirth, our family dynamics have never been more complicated. But there is something intriguing—and deeply comforting—about the idea that our love is recurring and eternal. And that our tiny babies could once have been our parents who were guiding us then, just as we now guide them.

▷ **That Magic Feeling**

Most of us are familiar with the term 'soul mates'—it's peppered through popular culture and our idea of fairy tale endings. Usually, we use it to refer to a romantic partner—someone we meet in a coffee shop and fall madly in love with. But the idea of a soul mate can go way beyond romantic chemistry. And, no, we don't only have one soul mate (that's just a product of our scarcity mindset).

The world-renowned psychotherapist Doctor Brian Weiss was astonished and sceptical when one of his patients began recalling past life traumas that seemed to hold the key to her recurring nightmares and anxiety attacks. His scepticism was eroded, however, when she began to channel messages from 'the space between lives', which contained revelations about Dr. Weiss' son who died at 23-days-old from a rare congenital heart condition.

This was the start of a new career phase for the psychotherapist, who went onto become a pioneer in past life healing. His book, *Only Love is Real,* documents how he helped two of his patients to realise that they had been lovers over centuries.

'In my research, I found we come back again and again with many of the same souls—soul mates or soul families,' writes Dr. Weiss in his book. 'The souls are the same, but the physical bodies change, and relationships change. For example, your grandmother can be your son—different physical form but the same soul.'[3]

This doesn't mean your relationship is always idyllic. According to Dr. Weiss, we collect as 'families of souls' because that's how we learn in this 'Earth School'. He adds, 'They know how to push our buttons; we know how to push theirs. We graduate together in families as souls.'

Perhaps, in this life, you choose to meet as siblings for the sake of supporting each other through a difficult childhood. Or you come together as business partners to create a product that makes the world better. It could also be a less dramatic reason, according to past life experts. Some of us just like to be around each other. After one lifetime we realise: 'You just make life feel better. Shall we do this again sometime?'

## ▷ The Soul Recognition Class

When you close your eyes, can you imagine your child's scent as a newborn? I sure can! The smell of the top of their head. Even the smell of their newborn nappies. I'm sure I could pick my kids out of a line-up from their odour alone. (Yes, including their gas!) According to past life experts, this could all be part of the masterplan. Whether you're meeting a life partner, a new bestie or coming skin-to-skin with your newborn, it's no coincidence that you seem to know them instantly. It's almost if … you were trained to recognise them.

Welcome to the weird and wonderful concept of the 'Soul Recognition Class'. This is the idea that, when we're in-between lives, we're all 'coached' on how to recognise our loved ones in the next lifetime.

According to Michael Armstrong, our past life messenger from a previous chapter, when people remember past life transitions, there are some commonalities in what they recall. When undergoing hypnosis, he says, many people recall a similar process in the 'in-between'. This is how Michael described it in a TikTok post on the topic:

> *Your view changes.* As a spirit, you see this reality [on earth] as a kind of simulation-like existence. You can float around in it and visit your memorial. When the time comes, they recall being guided to the spirit realm by

their spirit guide where they meet their 'soul family'. It sounds like the concept of a heaven.

*There is a 'Life Review'.* Imagine it like virtual reality goggles. You can go and look at anything from your life, revisit it and feel it. Did you utilise life to the best of your abilities? It's not done with judgement. But your soul does want the best for you. How can I do better in my next life?

*Choosing your next life.* They then describe choosing your next life for your greatest soul growth. This is your Soul Agreement. This includes choosing your parents, deciding whether to meet them and who is going to be your siblings.

*The Soul Recognition Class.* When you meet your soulmate, there is a certain aspect of them—how they look and smell—which helps you to recognise them. This is rehearsed over and over again, so you recognise them in your next life.

.... You're then brought into a baby's body to do it all over again.

Intrigued? I was! So, when I interviewed Michael, I had to ask about the Soul Recognition Class and what people seem to remember in their past life regressions. 'This happens just before you're about to come back,' explained Michael. 'You've chosen your life and your parents, where you're going to be born and when you're going to be born. You've made soul agreements with your friends and soul family. And then you do a Soul Recognition Class where essentially, over and over again, you practise recognising that soul in the scenario you're going to meet them.'

Of course, it can be easy to recognise our babies. For many women, they've just birthed them out of their body. One study found that 91 per cent of mothers could identify their newborn by olfactory clues after only 10 minutes of exposure to their newborn[4]. Likewise, a newborn can recognise the smell of their mum at only one day old. It makes sense, as this is the person who will feed you. But, if you believe in Soul Clusters, it goes way beyond a primitive survival strategy.

Michael gives the example of your best friend from school. 'When you cross paths, there has to be something you feel familiar with, that gets you to talk to them,' he says. 'A red sweater! In the Soul Recognition Class, you'll experience it over and over, so it imprints it on your soul. Red sweater. Red sweater. So, when it happens you get that soulmate, butterfly feeling.'

With your children, it could be even more subtle—their smell, the look in their eye, the shape of their face, the texture of their cheek. In my experience, it might not happen instantly. I felt an instant connection when my first daughter was born but, with my second child, I didn't get 'that' feeling for 10 long weeks. I remember clearly the moment when it felt like I 'knew' him. I was walking into the creche at my local gym. He was sitting on a carer's knee. I looked at his face and suddenly, the realisation hit home: I would do anything for this tiny human.

So, don't feel guilty if you're one of the (many) parents who didn't feel an instant connection to their children. It's more common than you think. Could it come down to your Soul Agreement? Maybe your souls agreed to wait a while. Maybe you practised for that moment to happen ten weeks after becoming a mother. We carry such guilt as parents if we don't feel an instant connection. But, is it really any different to knowing a platonic friend for years and then suddenly realising, they're the person of your dreams. Can we have a 'slow burn' with our baby, and still absolutely adore them? I'll never, ever forget the moment I locked eyes with my son—at 10 weeks old—and I fell in love. I don't think meeting any of my babies has been so magical.

Now, we've gone there, let's talk about another tough topic. Why it can feel so damn hard to love the people we love ... even if we believe that our souls were meant to come together.

## ▷ Pushing Our People Away

If you're someone who had an idyllic childhood, is in a dreamy marriage or feels at peace with your children, the idea of Soul Clusters is probably comforting and heart-warming. If you're juggling a difficult family dynamic, it can be less so—and it can bring up more questions than it answers.

- ▷ Why do I find it so hard to get on with these people?
- ▷ Why do I feel so triggered by my own family?
- ▷ Am I destined to repeat this struggle over and over?
- ▷ Am I a failure for ending a relationship with my soul mate?
- ▷ Why can't I let myself fall in love ... even with my own children?

First things first: even a soulmate relationship isn't always a 'forever' relationship. I'm not talking about your children here but, perhaps, with their biological mother or father—the person you created a life with. If you come back to the concept of Soul Contracts, it makes sense that some relationships are temporary and that, once you have fulfilled your agreement, it could be time to go in separate directions. So, please don't feel guilty if you've divorced or separated from the father or mother of your children. Trust, this is all part of your soul arrangement.

I've heard it said that, usually, when a soul relationship ends, both people start to realise it at the same time. (Rather than one person knowing and one person being shocked.) Both people have a deep knowing that their commitment has been completed.

When this happens, a lot of healers recommend doing a 'Cord Cutting Ritual'. This is a visualisation exercise where you imagine cutting the energetic cord that binds you to another person. (I have an audio recording of a cord cutting ritual on my website, *amymolloy.com.au/pastlifeparenting*.)

There are also times when we want to run away from a person, against our best interests. As a mother, I know that I have experienced times when all I wanted to do was to get in my car ... and keep driving, when the stress of juggling a household and the pain of loving so deeply simply felt too much. Maybe you too can relate to this. Even when we recognise a soul mate, or give birth to a child, we can push people away for a variety of reasons:

▷ Our past trauma.
▷ How parenting was modelled to us.
▷ Conditions like postnatal depression and postnatal anxiety.
▷ The stress of juggling work, parenting and keeping a roof over your head in a global financial crisis.

There are many factors that can harden us and put an emotional distance between us. As I write this, I've just gone through a period of pushing my husband away—my partner who I know, without question, is one of my soul mates. I'll share more in the chapter, *Healing Timelines* and how a 'repatterning exercise' helped me to come back to him, emotionally and sexually. For now, I just wanted to say—I'm no stranger to pushing people away. So, I'm writing this part of this chapter with no judgement and a heap of compassion.

Have you ever felt like it's hard to love even your own children? One of the reasons could be in your past life experiences. The past life hypnotist, Eli Bliliuos[5], who I previously spoke to about past life triggers, says a lot of his clients come to him for help with an intense relationship or attraction. 'They instantly recognise each other, And at the same time, they can trigger each other due to their shared history,' he says. This can show up in a fear of commitment, even to our own offspring.

'For example, maybe someone was orphaned in a past life,' says Eli. 'Maybe someone betrayed them. They're holding onto that and it's preventing them from connecting with others in the way they could. So, they had all this trauma from a past lifetime when they were left alone or this person wronged them. They don't want to get into a relationship because of that.'

Just as our earlier experiences in this life can prevent us from bonding with our loved ones, could our past life experiences also be at fault? Even if you deeply wanted a child, you could struggle to connect because of a past life imprint. 'I worked with a woman once,' says Eli. 'As a parent—a mother or father—in a past lifetime, she watched her child die. She came into this lifetime being very over-protecting. On the flip side, I worked with someone who had a similar experience yet didn't want to have anything to do with being a parent because of that experience. There are two sides to that coin.'

Through hypnosis, Eli worked with these women to form secure, loving connections. The first step is awareness, he says. Being aware of where our feelings come from can help us to reframe them and take back out power.

This is where I want to add a disclaimer: feeling a disconnection to your child can also be a sign of postnatal depression and postnatal anxiety, and help is available. (Please refer to the Appendix at the back of this book for support services.)

In addition, however, it can also be useful to look at your life in a very big picture. Are you holding back because you feel vulnerable? Do you have a fear of loss that's ingrained in you? Do you worry about what will happen if you 'let your walls down'? Is there a way you can normalise this fear?

For me, it helps to realise that every mother can feel vulnerable because of the deep love they feel for their babies. We don't have to fear that feeling. In fact, we can learn to accept and embrace it. When I feel scared about losing someone close to me, I rely on affirmations to reassure me. After giving birth to my third child, I carried a laminated piece of card in my pram that read:

*'We have a lifetime together.*
*We create health.*
*Our life will renew itself.*
*You can be the light.*
*Our babies make our life sparkle.'*

One of my life coaches, Katie Ford, calls it a 'grounding card' because it can stop you from floating away into what-ifs and catastrophising. It's a cliché, but, when we push someone away, it can be driven by a fear of loss or abandonment. We're protecting ourselves by getting ahead of the tragedy that might take them away from us. We would rather create a rift than be a victim to a rift happening.

If you're afraid of heartbreak, how can the concept of 'Soul Families' bring you comfort? For me, it has helped to ease my fear of death (more on this later.) If these people are 'my' people, I'm going to find them again, aren't I?

In his book, Dr. Weiss puts it like this: 'People grieve so much, which is understandable, as we lose loved ones. But, we're going to be reunited with those loved ones, either on the other side or back here in physical forms.' In working with his patients, this belief helps to transform grief. 'You still miss them but it's a different level, as you know you're coming back together,' he adds.

## ▷ The Science of Brand-New Souls

Before we move on, I want to briefly touch on brand-new souls. It doesn't appear to be common, but it does appear to happen—a soul that is here for the very first time. According to the past life experts that I interviewed, these souls are more likely to choose an 'easy' life, but that doesn't mean they're easy to parent—or to be married to. I was told, by multiple sources, that new souls often show up with common characteristics or attributes.

- ▷ Newer souls are usually focused more on money and 'shiny things'
- ▷ They can be more self-focused.
- ▷ They're usually extroverted and highly sociable.
- ▷ They like to be exposed to a wide variety of new ideas, hobbies and experiences.
- ▷ They are going to see the grey area less easily, so politics and controversial topics are going to be a hot topic for them.
- ▷ It's not uncommon for them to be agnostic or atheist.
- ▷ They're often one step ahead of emerging trends and highly innovative.
- ▷ They're competitive because they're all about finding their place in the world.

▷ Usually, they have good health in their younger year and a well-balanced body.

▷ They can struggle with the cause-and-effect concept, and struggle with why certain things keep happening to them.

In children who are new souls, the characteristics are even more specific:

▷ As kids, they can be hyper-active and seem to have endless energy.

▷ They might get in trouble for talking too much or too loudly.

▷ They love meeting new people, the more the better.

▷ They're curious and interested in all spiritual practices.

▷ They often reject formal education to follow their own path.

▷ They revel in creative pursuits.

▷ They have a passion for novelty and often reject traditions.

▷ Generally, they have an energy that can feel hard to keep up with

Think of a new soul as your mate who hasn't been to therapy. They're fun to be around, they have boundless energy and they're the life of the party. But, they can also be a little 'too much' for some people, especially people who don't understand them. In my experience, it's great to have a mixture of old and new souls in a family. Do you have it in yours?

A few weeks ago, my six-year-old daughter announced that her soul is 'brand spanking new'. She doesn't believe that she's been here before, although she believes she will have more lives in the future. I'm not saying whether she's right or wrong, but she does seem to move through life with a lightness, a joyfulness and a deep sense of wonder. My husband is the same, whereas I've definitely done a few rounds in 'Earth School'. Perhaps, that's why we work so well together.

## Chapter 5 ▷ Thinking Points

▷ Can you think of a time you had an instant recognition with someone, perhaps your partner, a friend or a mentor. Can you remember a moment of incredible recognition and belonging?

▷ Take a moment to be grateful for the people in your life—your 'soul family'—who feel like they were sent to guide you or evolve you as a person.

▷ How can you offer yourself more compassion for the relationships that have ended in your life, by realising that, even soul contracts, don't have to be forever.

▷ Do you recognise any 'new souls' in your life? Remember, all our kids are different, and comparison isn't helpful to anyone. Embrace their uniqueness.

# PART 2: PARENTING WITH PRESENCE

*I believe there are all these worlds happening at the same time. They're all connected so one world impacts the other world. And I'm going to do something in this world that saves another world.*

Hazel, aged 7

# Chapter 6:
# Big Feelings & Real Meanings

*What does your family's nervous system need?*

▷ When I was researching this book, one topic kept coming up again and again: why do some kids (and adults!) feel everything so very deeply? Whether I was talking about parents, children, triggers, or attachment styles in relationships, one word kept popping up in my research: empathy. What does it mean to be an empathic person growing up in this weird, wild world? Is there a link between empaths and children with past life memories?

The answer to the second question is yes, according to Peter Smith, the founder of the Institute for Quantum Consciousness. Previously an executive in the Australian banking system, a series of events led him to train under the spiritual hypnotherapist, Doctor Michael Newtown. He ended up as the President of The Michael Newton Institute for Life Between Lives Hypnotherapy. Since then, Peter has worked with adults and children across the globe to unlock past life memories, explore experiences of the afterlife and even delve into their future. He says that the latest generation of kids are different—and it's a great thing for our planet. 'What I'm finding, if I'm looking at the kids coming through, is two trends,' says Peter. 'Kids are coming through with increased sensitivities and more natural metaphysical connections, which means, to me, the veil is getting thinner.'[1]

In a later chapter, I'll go into Peter's knowledge of 'off-planet' reincarnation. (Yes, I'm talking about children reincarnating from different planets.) For now, let's focus on the link between kids who can remember past lives and kids who are empaths. 'A lot of these kids are energetically sensitive,' explains Peter. 'I've worked with little kids who've picked up difficult family situations between mum and dad. I worked with a kid who took on the sadness of an entire funeral. A lot of these kids don't do what other kids do. They're rebelling in the school system. They can be labelled as 'bad' children.'

In Peter's experience, these so-called 'bad' kids are great healers. In fact, they hold an important place in the world's uplevelling. 'My take, from what I've been told by clients, is there is an awakening happening here,' he says. 'We carry a very heavy collective memory of humanity from all the horrible things that have happened in history. People are incarnating deliberately into family lines in order to have access to trauma so we can clear it.'

So, if your sensitive child triggers you, reframe it as a positive. They're shining a light on your own tough stuff, so that you can start to heal it. (We'll go into how in great detail in Part 3, *Reparenting Yourself*.) And that can have a ripple effect on society, and beyond.

## ▷ Where Do Feelings Come From?

If you're a parent with a Highly Sensitive Child (or you're part of a Highly Sensitive Family), this chapter probably caught your attention. We've all had that head-in-hands moment when our child has a meltdown or we snap at them out of frustration. Most parents are adept at blaming themselves and wondering what we did 'wrong', but could there be another reason? Are they just feeling the world more deeply than most people and what are the positives?

The term 'empath' comes from the word empathy—the ability to understand the experiences and feelings of people outside of your own perspective. In the spiritual sense, it goes one step further—it describes a person with the ability to feel the mental, emotional, or even physical state of another individual. According to psychologists, empaths—in the traditional sense—are both born and created. It appears, some children are born more sensitive. It can also be inherited if you have a sensitive parent as a role model.

The good news is, that same parent, the sensitive one, can also become a lighthouse, teaching a sensitive child how to find shelter and how to shine their own light. Judith Orloff, the author of *The Empaths Survival Guide*[2] puts it like this: 'Parents are powerful role models for all children, especially sensitive ones.'

I am the perfect mother for my son because we share many of the same attributes, including his beautiful sensitivities. The problem is that our world, and our school system, is not really set up for empaths. As children, we're taught to be available, open and cooperative; to sit in large halls of students and to always be eager and willing. That's not a bad thing, but it's all about balance. An empath child also needs to be taught how to set self-supporting emotional boundaries. And how to energetically say, 'No, I don't want to feel what you're feeling. Not today. You can be you and I can be me.'

When Peter works with empath adults, many of whom remember past lives, he guides them to install three new 'protocols' in their subconscious. These are:

▷ to observe and not absorb,

▷ to know what's, yours and what is somebody else's; and

▷  absolute, total, and complete permission to exercise energetic discernment.

This isn't about not feeling anything; it's about feeling your *own* feelings and only feeling other people's feelings when (and only when) it has positive benefits. If you're an empath, you can feel like emotional flypaper, attracting and getting stuck to every emotion in your vicinity. But there is an alternative ...

As a father, Peter practises 'energetic discernment' with his grown-up daughter. 'All empaths need to put a system in place,' he says. 'My daughter lives in London and works in the mental health field as a caseworker, so she's in bad energy all the time. I say to her, 'Have you been using the tools I offered you? When did you last clear your energy field?' She needs different ways to move through the world and look after herself.'

As kids, we're taught to brush our teeth, wash our hands, and clean our face. But are we taught about 'energetic hygiene'? This is the idea that we can all take steps to remove the energetic grime of the day and refresh our energy fields.

One of the mums that I interviewed gives her daughter an 'energy bath' every night. After they wash themselves with soap in the bath, they also imagine washing the energy field around their body. (She says, her daughter loves this ritual!)

Currently, before my six-year-old daughter goes to sleep, I cleanse her energy with the Peruvian perfume, Agua De Florida—one of the main colognes used in South America by shamans as a spiritual tool for ceremonial protection, cleansing and healing. (I sell the cologne on my website when I have stock available.)

After she lays down under her blankets, I rub the perfume between my palms and move them above her body, from the top of her head to her toes.

I'm clairsentient, which means I can have the ability to feel the past, present and future emotional state of other people. If I'm honest, I feel like we all have this ability with our own children, especially when they're under the age of seven. (It's said, mothers and their children share a chakra system until a child is seven years old.)

When I wave my hands over my kid's energy fields, I can feel areas of heaviness, cloudiness or shadow, and I can shift it. I trust my mother's intuition and wave it away like I'm wafting smoke; or I use incense and sage to smudge the area around them. (Side note: I make sure I wash my hands thoroughly or have a shower afterwards so I'm not walking around with their foggy energy.)

Now, my six-year-old will asks me, 'Mummy, can I cleanse my energy?' She has a little bottle of Agua De Florida on her bedside table, which she uses to clear the energy around her elephant comforter and her unicorn stuffed animal.

Meanwhile, my three-year-old will wander around with a burning sage stick. (My kids are very capable with fire safety.) And they all sleep with cut up limes beside their beds. The Australian medium, Jessica Lynne, who I interviewed for an article I wrote for *Marie Claire* on the rise of psychics, says it keeps negative spirits away and helps your kids sleep. (I'll do anything to get my kids to sleep through the night.)

To me, this is how we change the world in one generation: by teaching children that, not only can they cleanse their own energy, but, when they choose to, they can shift the emotions of other people. So often we can feel like a victim in the world, powerless to the changing mood of society, but I want to change this for my children. I want them to see, an energy shift is always possible.

## ▷ Over-Feeling Children in a Fearful World

Let's be honest, parenting an empath child can feel like a lot of hard work. Parenting when you're an empath can feel even harder! Put the two together and you're in trouble. Parenting is a highly-stimulating job, as is going to school or childcare or playdates for our children. But, that's only because we've never been given the tools and taught the techniques to protect our own energy, without taking on the feelings of the masses.

In a previous chapter, I introduced you to the medium and energy healer, Dana Childs. She is also the creator of the course, *Empowered Empath* and an expert on the topic of empath children. I asked her whether being an empath is a good or a bad thing? 'A lot of people answer that depending on where they are in their empathic journey,' says Dana. 'If you are an empath and it's ruling your life, it's going to be a bad thing: I can't go to concerts; I feel everyone's stuff. It's going to do a number on you. If you're empowered and learn healthy boundaries, being an empath is so helpful.'

In her previous career, Dana worked as a schoolteacher, working with teenagers. As an empath herself, she really began noticing her gift when it came to her relationships with her students. She knew the names of kids she'd never met before. She could pick up on issues happening in her student's home lives. She earned the nickname 'the teacher with eyes in the back of her head'. She thinks back on that time lovingly and says, 'I just had the ability to know what was needed.'

As a former 'empath school teacher', she says one of the most important tools to teach kids is how to trace where their feelings really come from. (Let's remember that empath kids can adopt other people's emotions and physical symptoms). You can follow a script like this, says Dana:

*'You have a tummy ache?*

*What does that tummy ache feel like?*

*Do you think it's an emotion or a thought?*

*Did you get that tummy ache at school?*

*Were you around someone when you got that tummy ache?*

*If it was two days in a row, were you around the same person?*

*Do you think it's someone else's tummy ache?'*

The idea is, we only need to take responsibility for the feelings that are ours to process. 'You're teaching the intention that you're not going to 'feel, deal or heal' energy that doesn't belong to you,' adds Dana. She teaches kids and parents an energy protection technique called 'The satellite dish.' Imagine a satellite dish sitting against your body, as if it's resting against your hips or your belly. The energy coming at you hits the satellite dish and is sent back outwards. It's a great visualisation to use in busy spaces or moments of confrontation.

It's similar to a technique taught to me by Peter Smith, which I've gone on to teach to my own little ones. When a child is upset, gently ask them a series of questions, which go something like this:

*'So, you're angry. Feel into that. Does this feel like yours or someone else's anger?'*

*'Oh, it might be someone else's.'*

*'Close your eyes and find out what it is.'*

*'Oh, it's Wendy, we had a fight at school today.'*

*'Okay, close your eyes and let all of Wendy's energy go up into the universe, and send her love, because that's what you can do.'*

The key with empathic kids, according to Peter, is to coach them to 'send rather than absorb'. Send back energy that doesn't belong to you. Send good thoughts. Send nice things. 'When an empath child is distressed, they don't need to be told to quit crying,' says Peter. 'They need to be understood. You have an energy field, and your energy is a little disrupted at the moment. Let's work out where it's coming from and see what we can do about it.'

Like most parenting practises, checking in with our own nervous system is important. Do you feel anxious when you drop your kids at school? Do your stress levels rise when you're in the playground waiting for pick-up? Personally, I didn't have a great experience when I was at Catholic school in England and, when my son started kindergarten, I noticed that my old fears were being activated. Every time I entered the school, I felt under threat. (It was nothing to do with him, he loved it there.) I quickly realised, I needed to address my school sensitivities, before my son picked up on them.

It was one of my spiritual mum friends who recommended that I 'blast the school with positive energy'. The next time I collected my kids from school, I sat in my car and practised a visualisation. I imagined angels standing at the four corners of the building. They were smiling and happy and laughing and filling the school with a bright, white light. I asked them to protect my kids and to lift the entire school's vibration.

From that day, I didn't feel any of the heaviness I previously felt whenever I stepped onto school grounds. It also helped that, instead of waiting in the sterile playground, I found a lovely, little garden to wait for my children. Now, I look forward to hanging out there in the sunshine before the school bell rings.

This is how you take responsibility for your own sensitivities, and how to ripple it to your children. (Because I know, they know, I'm in a better mood when I collect them.) This brings me perfectly to our next topic ...

## ▷ Can you Cosmically Heal as a Family?

The Australian energy healer, Justine Sharkie has a child who feels things—a lot. 'My daughter is 10 and she's an amazing specimen,' says Justine, speaking of the oldest of her three children. 'People can't believe her wisdom and how she articulates ideas. But, from a young age, she could also get very angry and that really triggered me, as I was never allowed to be angry when I was younger. I felt like an unsafe little girl whenever she was angry.'[3]

Justine is no stranger to the world of past lives and shadow work. With a background in psychology and psychotherapy, her first job was working as a school counsellor before her own 'spiritual awakening'. Today, she is an energy healer and cosmic channel, and the creator of *The Witch Wounds* course. It explores the ways that we, as women, have been suppressed and repressed (both in this lifetime and previous lifetimes). I've completed *Witch Wounds* and it was incredible—I highly recommend it.

To create more harmony in her home, Justine has done 'the work' herself, studying meditation and kinesiology, going to countless retreats and exploring past life regressions. It has been helpful, she says, but she also finds great healing in everyday parenting moments. 'All of us are always healing light-years of shadow work in every moment,' says Justine. 'I don't even think of it now. It's just ingrained in our family. We're working multi-dimensionally every day.'

That sounds great, but what does it look like, exactly? 'The key, which I keep coming back to, is presence,' explains Justine. 'You don't need to get crystals out and pray at the moon. It's always happening—you can't actually *not* be doing past life healing.'

The night before our interview, she had been watching the Disney movie, *Encanto* with her daughters. It's the story of a girl in a magical family, who is searching for her own mystical power, but who feels like an outcast. 'I felt an absolute soul-level healing through that movie,' says Justine. 'In my meditation the day before, I had felt like I was standing on a threshold. I was standing at a door, saying to my guides, 'I just don't know what I need. What's the healing?' In that meditation, there was no breakthrough. I got nothing.'

Fast-forward to the following day ... She started bawling her eyes out, watching the end of the movie when (spoiler alert!) the little girl discovers her true power, cheered on by her family. 'It felt like a permission slip for me,' adds Justine. 'It was a big release for me and my children. I didn't need to explain to them. My release is their release. Their release is my release. I felt like we all moved through something together.'

It would be easy to overlook moments like these in the mishmash of parenting moments, but even a simply ritual like walking with your kids on the beach or laying in the garden can become more than that. As Justine says, 'Life is giving you opportunities to heal as a family in every moment. Just be aware of it.'

Part of raising an empathic child is constantly reminding yourself that they are far more capable than you can give them credit for. This is something my husband reminds me, frequently, when I'm worried about my little boy's first visit to the dentist; how he'll cope at a busy music festival; whether he will handle a new change or transition. In the end, I always underestimate his abilities, and he is constantly astounding me. This is part of past life parenting—the realisation that our kids are incredibly capable and resilient in their own way.

Today, Justine says her oldest daughter, who is now a tween, can hold her own in the busy world. In her free time, she reads self-development books and she is exploring her own past life healing. When she feels activated, she watches an Autonomous Sensory Meridian Response (ASMR) video on YouTube. Like millions of people across the world, she finds it relaxing to watch videos of people whispering, spraying water or crinkling wrapping paper.

Justine has learnt to guide her sensitive child, but also to trust her. Yes, you can nudge your child to explore meditation or breathing exercise, but they might also find their own route to regulation. Our job, as a past life parent, is to teach our children to embrace and accept themselves, even their own limitations. And to find imaginative ways to support themselves.

'After [my daughter] turned seven, there was this real shift,' says Justine. 'At the time, our relationship was still very triggering. I didn't feel like I was doing a great job as a mum. I remember, on her seventh birthday, getting this download that said, 'You've done it.' I knew, in that moment, I'd done everything energetically to move her forward. I felt a deep sense of peace.'

## Chapter 6 ▷ Thinking Points

▷ How can we shift our thinking that a highly sensitive child is a problem? In fact, empathic kids are here to help heal the world and raise our vibration.

▷ Empathic kids (and adults) can pick up on other people's emotions and physical symptoms—so try to trace that tummy ache!

▷ When a big feeling comes up, the question to ask is: is this my feeling? If it isn't, the good news is, you can let go of it.

▷ Don't put sensitivity on your goal list to change or cure!

▷ If you want to cosmically heal your family, just try to be present. Past life healing is always happening—even on family movie night.

▷ You might like to try this parenting affirmation: 'My creative brain will always find a solution.' Teach this affirmation to your little ones too.

# Chapter 7:
# What Did We Sign Up For?

*What if you just promised to be present for it all?*

▷ When I was writing this book, my friend, Meagan Donaldson sent me a text with unexpected news. Halfway through her pregnancy with her son, Remy, he had passed away, 15 minutes after being born. For Meagan and her husband, Chris, this was their second infant loss. Their first child, Violet, was stillborn a few years earlier—the result of two different, unconnected medical conditions.

I had met Meagan a few months after Violet's death, when she decided to write a book based on her experience of saying goodbye to her daughter. I had the honour of editing her book, *Still a Mum*, whilst I was pregnant with my third baby. (It was emotional!) Since then, her book has helped parents across the world to heal and has even changed the way the medical system and funeral sector support grieving families. (Side note: I didn't include a trigger warning on this chapter after speaking to parents in the infant loss community. Many parents who've lost a child think it's disrespectful to have to warn people before talking about their children.)

After Violet's death, Meagan created the fundraising campaign, *Violet's Gift*, in her daughter's memory. With the money raised, she created a special labour room in the hospital where Violet was born—a calming space for mothers to say goodbye to their babies. She also purchased two Cuddle Cots for the hospital—cooling systems that fit into a small cot, which allow families to spend more time with their deceased baby. She never predicted that, three years later, she would birth her son in the room she created. Or place his body in the Cuddle Cot to take him home to meet his one living sibling.

It's fair to say that Meagan is one of the bravest, kindest and kick-arse mothers I know. So, why did this happen to her again? It's a question that Meagan also asked herself, especially in the early days. 'A week after Remy died, I was seeking reassurance, listening to lots of podcasts about signs and connections to spirits,' says Meagan. 'Someone had recommended a medium who they thought was great, so I listened to their podcast.'

Amongst a lot of advice, which she did resonate with, the medium shared their thoughts on recurring trauma. One of the theories they shared was that people who experience the same life-changing or altering trauma, usually experience it because they haven't learnt from it the first time. 'My brain instantly went: what more could I have possibly learnt?' says Meagan. 'I wrote a book; I raised money for charity; I created a room in a hospital. I have changed as a person and changed my life purpose based on my trauma. So, why on earth were we here again?'

Whether or not you believe in rebirth, we can all relate to this thought-spiral. When something bad happens, we want someone or something to blame. We want to join the dots back to what we could have done, and forward, to how this will help us in the future. We are the generation who have been raised on the adage, 'What doesn't kill you makes you stronger.' But, that's an over-simplified statement; one which doesn't bring much comfort and doesn't come close to explaining the complexities of karma. We all want to know: why is this happening to us—and are we strong enough to survive it? And never is this truer than those heartbreaking moments when something happens to one of our children.

## ▷ Breaking Down Karma

When we think of karma, our mind usually goes to the Hollywood interpretation: If we're a 'baddie' in this life, we'll come back as a bug. If we're a 'goodie', we'll come back as a princess or maybe a butterfly. In reality, the religions that do believe in karma don't see it so simply. In fact, it's a hotly debated topic, even (especially) in the Buddhist community. Some religious scholars believe that it's an outdated-concept, and that we should do away with it completely. Which feels like good news for parents who already have enough guilt to deal with! So, let's start with the more traditional idea of karma and break down some common misconceptions.

According to Buddhist teachings, karma (or *kamma*) is not a moral judgement, nor is it a reward or a punishment. It's simply a matter of cause-and-effect or, in layman's terms, 'like attracting like'. If you do good deeds, you get good results; if you do bad deeds, you get bad results. In Buddhism, karma isn't decided by a god-like figure. As the Buddhist monk and scholar, Sayadaw U Silananda explains[1]: 'These good and bad results are not given by anyone and are not given as reward and punishment. Kamma is a moral law, which needs no lawgiver, a law which operates naturally.'

It's worth noting that karma isn't blamed for everything. In Buddhism, there are 24 'conditions', which are said to affect the reality we experience, and karma is only one of them. Plus, you can escape karma. In Buddhism, karma is not an action, it's a 'mental urge', which lead to an action or outcome to happen. The theory is, if we can become mindful enough, we can change even our deepest karma and not act on those urges.

As someone raised with the Catholic idea of heaven and hell, I must admit, that this is where you start to lose me. It can sound like a doctrine, peddled to keep us in check, especially if you identify as female. This feels especially true when you investigate the Hindu concept of karma, which is largely linked to the ideas of desire (sexual and appetite). When you desire anything for yourself (whether it's a quickie or a croissant), it creates karma, because you don't have selfless intentions. Because of this, some *Swami* (Hindu teachers), say that the goal is to be reborn without any sexual desires[2].

As the mother of daughters, who I hope embrace their passions, I'm not sure that I can buy into this premise. In fact, I'm tempted to say, 'bring it on' to a lifetime of karmic retribution, if it allows my children to eat carbohydrates and bring themselves to orgasm. I certainly don't want to raise my daughters to be terrified of (very normal!) emotions like anger because they think it's going to make them 'ugly' (which is one of the religious karmic teachings!). Or, to worry that a touch of jealousy will damn them to a lifetime of loneliness.

Even the idea of 'cleansing' your karma feels like it's a recipe for mum-guilt. As a parent, I instantly think: 'So, if something happens to me or my kids, it's because I didn't make enough effort to clean up my karma.' I can't help thinking of parents like Meagan, who could be tempted to blame themselves for heartbreaking tragedies and the loss of their babies. I do, however, understand the appeal of karma. As humans, we love to feel in control and the mechanical nature of cause-and-effect can seem appealing ('if I am good, I will receive goodness' etc). Part of the process of grieving is finding meaning and re-ordering our toughest moments to make sense of them. So, if it's not karma, how can we explain the tragedies and challenges that we do face in life? The answer could lie in the concept of Soul Contracts ...

## ▷ Soul Contracts & Conscious Choices

If you've spent any time in the spiritual space, you'll probably have heard of the idea of 'soul contracts'. To put it simply, it's the idea that, before we enter this body, we agree to a set of commitments and promises. In this vein, there is a pre-existing plan for our lives, including many of our relationships, challenges and victories. It can be a comforting concept, especially when life feels out of control. If you believe that you agreed to all of this beforehand you can go from feeling like a passive victim to an empowered instigator. I remember when my youngest child was born during the Covid lockdown, taking a lot of comfort from this premise.

> *Old way of thinking:* What am I doing, birthing this poor baby into a world that's in chaos?

> *New way of thinking:* She chose to be born into lockdown. She knows exactly what she's doing. She wants this. She chose us. She came here to spend the pandemic together.

In my experience, most past life experts agree on one thing: our children choose us as parents. From the 'in between'—the space between lives—they see us, warts and all. They are aware of our flaws, our history. And of course, all our good points. As we covered in our chapter on Soul Clusters, our children choose us, knowing our past and our future. By taking this view, there are no 'accidental' pregnancies—only conscious connections.

So, let's discuss how this relates to personal challenges and setbacks. For example, if your child gets sick, or you get sick; if you don't have enough money to buy them an iPad; if they're bullied at school because of their accent; or any number of challenges which break our hearts as parents. If you believe in soul contracts, then you choose to believe that you—and your child—were aware that this would happen. Many people also believe that soul contracts are designed to teach us about humanity. According to this idea, when we are born, we inherit a family with a goal of learning a lesson or of raising its vibration.

I appreciate, this is a hard pill to swallow if you come from a history of family violence or if you were mistreated by your parents. I'm not going to be the one to tell you to find peace with it—that might just not be possible. But I will share the opinion of Peter Smith, founder of the Institute for Quantum Consciousness, who says, 'People are incarnating deliberately into family lines in order to have access to the trauma so we can clear it.'

For example, you could choose to reincarnate into a family because you will be the person to end a cycle of trauma. This could mean learning from your parents how *not* to parent and parenting your own children in a different way. When you're faced with such a challenge, how can you look for the lesson:

*'What does my soul have to learn from this?'*

*'Why would I have agreed to this?'*

*'How could this possibly be a positive lesson, for me personally and/ or for humanity?'*

It can sound very grandiose but, if we believe in soul contracts, these are the kinds of questions we can gently ponder. Because it's not just only about our individual soul experience, it's about the furthering of the human race (go us!). Does that mean we have to like it? Hell no!

The American medium, Laura Lynn Jackson is quick to point out that we can sign a soul contract, land here on earth and still have a 'what did I do?' moment. But everything we experience is a 'lesson is love' and, therefore, in our best interest. In her book, *Signs: The Secret Language of the Universe*, she writes:

*'It has been said that people cross our paths and enter our lives as either a blessing or a lesson. Often, it is both. Either they have something to teach us, or we have something to teach them, or, at best, we have something to teach each other. That is how this great chain of light and interconnection works.'*

When I spoke to my friend Meagan about these ideas, we both agreed: you can see the lessons you've learnt from a loss ... and it can still suck! 'I've been given so many gifts from Violet and Remy,' says Meagan. 'I'm an even more empathetic person now, a better friend and family member. It's turned up the light in all aspects of my life ... but I would give all of that back if I could have my three children here with me. I'd choose that again and again.'

During one of our phone conversations, I floated an idea to Meagan. What if this soul contract was about Remy, not her? Her son had chosen her knowing that his time in this lifetime would be very short. He chose her knowing that she would have the courage to be with him; to hold him for the 15 minutes that he was breathing. To courageously watch him pass away without looking away.

Later that night, Meagan sent me a text: 'I can't stop thinking about the idea that maybe Remy's experience wasn't about me, but him. That brings me immeasurable comfort.' There is no way of knowing for sure right now. As Laura Lynn Jackson says, sometimes we don't find out a 'why' until we get to the other side. But, we also have to trust our mother's instincts—and that felt true for Meagan.

Less than a month later, Meagan called me again. A few weeks after Remy died, her beloved Nana had also died. Then she was told, the urn she'd ordered for Remy had gotten lost in the post. That meant that his ashes had to stay at the funeral home longer than expected. In fact, he was still there when her Nana also arrived.

'I chose Remy's funeral director because she had read my book,' says Meagan. 'She contacted me after she read it and said, 'it's changed the way we work with families.' After Remy died, I knew it had to be her, as she really seemed to care.' And she did care. In fact, after Meagan's Nana was also brought to the funeral home, the director sent Meagan a message: 'Is it okay if I place Remy in her arms?'

Of course, Meagan said yes. 'So, his little ashes were actually in my nana's arms in the funeral home,' she says. 'It's so hard, so deep, so heavy and so beautiful.'

If the funeral director hadn't read Meagan's book, maybe she wouldn't have even sent that message, or had the compassion to create that special moment. That's the great chain of light and interconnection. These are the moments that raise all our vibrations, and give us hope that love always wins.

## ▷ Intergenerational Trauma

As I write this, Intergenerational Trauma is a hot button topic—the idea that trauma can be 'passed down' through a family member to the next generations. Maybe you've felt it or maybe you're currently trying to break a cycle (isn't every generation?). Of course, in an ideal world, we don't want to pass any trauma onto to our children. But, that's probably not possible. I joke that my children are going to end up in therapy—I just hope it's for a different reason than I am! What a waste it will be for me to do all this work, only for them to still be dealing with it.

When it comes to karma, everyone seems to disagree on whether you can 'inherit' your parent's karmic baggage. A quick Google search brings up plenty of articles offering advice on how to 'clear your family karma'. But it was the Buddha who apparently said, 'We are the heirs of our own actions', suggesting that only we create our karma and, therefore, our future.

There is also the spiritual belief that, until the age of seven, a child shares their mother's chakras—the energy system which runs through our body. Certain events or traumas can 'block' our chakras and, therefore, our energy. Until the age of seven, a child is thought to be tied to their mother's energy, and any blocks that mothers have are also felt by the child[3]. The theory goes that if a child under the age of seven experiences an illness, it is not because of their karma, but is a reflection of that parent's karma[4]. (Although, I'm reluctant to write that, as mothers already find enough reasons to feel guilty.)

Let's bring it back to science for a moment. You may have heard of the emerging field of epigenetics—the study of how your behaviours and environment can cause changes that affect the way that your genes work. During development, the DNA that makes up our genes accumulates chemical marks that determine how much or little of the genes is expressed. This collection of chemical marks is known as the 'epigenome'.[5]

It turns out, our epigenome can be affected by positive experiences, such as supportive relationships, but also by negative experiences and trauma. This explains why genetically identical twins can exhibit different behaviours, skills, health and achievement. And it can affect future generations. One study found that children of pregnant women who experienced famine carried a specific chemical marker—or an 'epigenetic signature'—on one of their genes. Researchers later linked this epigenetic signature to differences in health later in life, including higher-than-average body mass.[6] Another study found that generations of mice seemed to inherit a fear-response to the scent of cherry blossom. It was linked back to an epigenetic modification in their smell receptor.

This is a long-winded way to say: what our parents experience does influence us. And it doesn't feel like too much of a leap to imagine that our past lives might also be as impactful. We're not only inheriting our parent's trauma—could we also inherit our own trauma from a previous lifetime? Over the next five to ten years, it's expected we will see rapid progress in research around epigenetics. Perhaps, even by the time you read this book, we'll have a clear understanding of generational trauma and its impact.

For now, I want to put a more positive spin on intergenerational trauma; to offer hope to every parent, especially women, who feels the weight of 'breaking a cycle'. If intergenerational pain is that powerful, then so is intergenerational peace and happiness. Yes, our negative bias makes us worry more about the bad stuff, but have you ever thoughts about focusing on how your children can inherit your happiness? It's a mindset shift that I'm currently exploring and it's working.

Here's the thing: I could spend the next twenty years trying to be a 'cycle breaker' or I could focus on being a 'cycle starter'. I could hyper-focus on shielding my children from my past pain, or I could role-model the benefits of 'Post traumatic growth' (PTG). Research shows that, in the aftermath of adversity, we can actually see improvements in multiple areas of our life: personal strengths, spiritual change, our relationship with others and overall life appreciation. Now, that's a cycle I'm happy to welcome my children into.

So, for the parent who thinks they're messing up their kids—or believes that their karma is going to be felt by future generations—just have faith. We all inherited a touch of trauma, whether it was from our World War grandparents or our own inner battles. With every tragedy, there is an opportunity for growth, and our kids get to discover that too.

## Chapter 7 ▷ Thinking Points

▷ Even in the traditional idea of karma, it isn't blamed for everything that happens in life—so don't blame yourself.

▷ When you're faced with a challenge, how can you look for the lesson: What does my soul need to learn from this?

▷ How can you 'learn from love' in a challenging experience?

▷ Can you look back, join the dots of your life, and start to understand why an event happened? How can this bring you comfort?

▷ Can you reframe your role from cycle breaker to cycle starter? How can appreciate your own post traumatic growth, so your children can reap the benefits too?

# Chapter 8:
# **Attachment & Trust**

*It is all sacred. Every school drop-off. Every swimming lesson. Every bath time. Every moment of peace after bedtime. It is all divine.*

Of all the interviews I did for this book, none stuck with me more than mother of two, Anita Kaushal. It was one of those soul-changing conversations you find yourself thinking about late at night, talking about to your friends and locking into your subconscious.

Born and raised in West London, Anita grew up steeped in her family's Indian heritage. Although she had been brought up with the idea of reincarnation, it didn't become significant until her daughter, Milli was diagnosed with an inoperable brain tumour. Milli was two years old when she was first diagnosed and, although treatment was initially successful, when she was 10 years old, it was found the cancer had returned. This time, her parents were told there was nothing they could do to save her.

At this point, Anita and her husband, Bittu, had to make a heartbreaking decision: should they tell their 10-year-old daughter that she was dying? In an interview for Mo Gawdat's podcast, Slo Mo, Anita recalled the moment. 'I remember saying to my husband

"I want to tell Milli she's leaving,'" says Anita. 'As a Hindu, I believe in reincarnation—we reincarnate every morning from our sleep, and I feel [death] is no different. I didn't want her to go into her next life feeling mistrust. So, as her mother, I felt a duty to tell her the truth.'

One of Anita's friends gave her this advice: 'Tell her that God wants her to wear a new costume and play a new part in the drama'. So, this is how Anita explained reincarnation to her dying daughter: 'Darling, I just think God wants you to play a new part in the drama. Maybe you get to be a princess. You get to be whatever you want to be. But, maybe it's time to play a new part.'

She also told Milli a story about her toy bunny and how she could 'travel through the light' to be reunited with her friends and family. 'She was sad, and we hugged, she cried, and I cried, and then there was an asceptance, and the fear seemed to diminish,' adds Anita.

At the age of 11, Milli died, two weeks after Anita's father passed away unexpectedly in his sleep. By this point, Milli had lost her sight and speech, but the last thing she did was to silently tap her thumb and then two fingers on the bed. It was code for 'I love you'.

When I interviewed Anita, it had been over 10 years since Milli's transition from this life. I asked her if she had any regrets about choosing an honest approach? 'Would [Milli] have felt better if we had lied? I can never know that, but I did what felt right at the time,' says Anita. 'We did not dwell on it, but we reached a point of acceptance. I think children are wiser than we give them credit for, and she was certainly my teacher.'

Her beliefs around reincarnation also drove her decision. 'I believe, the personality does take residue from past lives,' adds Anita. 'I did not want Milli to leave this incarnation with mistrust.

I felt it was unkind for her to see herself physically diminished and for us to be telling her otherwise.'[1]

Later in this chapter, we'll come back to Milli's story and how her parents have managed to ease their pain with trust, despite missing her. I want to say thank-you to Anita and her family, as they very rarely do interviews discussing Milli's death. In this instance, they were happy to share with the hope that their story would bring comfort to other families.

It's fair to say that it's every parent's worst nightmare, the thought of losing a child, but does it have to be? Is there any way that we can navigate parenthood without such a chronic fear of loss? And how can we better prepare our kids for a world where we can't always be with them?

## ▷ Can Our Kids Trust Us?

The social scientist Brené Brown talks a lot about trust, as well as her expert subject, vulnerability. According to Brené, trust, whether it's with our children, our peers, or our partners, is built in small, everyday moments, which set us up to be ready for larger struggles.

She began researching the topic of trust after a conversation with her young daughter who was struggling to know who to trust in her friendship group. 'One day, my daughter Ellen, came home from school in third grade,' recalls Brené in an interview for Oprah's Supersoul Sessions. 'The minute we closed the front door, she started sobbing and slid down the door, until she was a heap on the floor. It scared me.'[2]

When she was able to talk, her daughter explained that she had confided in two friends who then told the whole class her 'secret'. When she returned to the classroom, it felt like all her classmates were pointing, calling her names and laughing at her. She looked at her mum and said, 'I will never trust anyone again'.

As a mother, Brené's first reaction was protective: 'Damn straight, you don't tell anyone anything, but your mama.' But, she knew that this wasn't the answer. So, she came up with the 'marble jar' analogy. At the time, her daughter's teacher used a marble jar as a teaching tool. If the kids made good decisions together, the teacher added a marble to the jar. If they made poor decisions, a marble was taken away. When the marble jar was full, the class enjoyed a celebration.

This is how Brené chose to explain trust: 'Ellen, trust is like a marble jar. You share those hard stories and hard things happening to you with friends who, over time, fill up a marble jar. They've done thing after thing after thing until you know—I can trust this person.'

Since then, she has worked with The Gottman Institute, which specialises in relationships, to delve further into the topic of trust in families and beyond. The evidence is clear: trust is built in the smaller moments. And never is this truer than with our children. Yes, we opened this chapter with a huge, terrible truth—telling your child that they have a terminal illness. But, to get to that point of total trust and honesty we must build a trusting foundation ... brick by brick, by brick. So, what is a brick even made of?

▷ When your kids tell you a secret and you don't jump to judge them.

▷ When your kid is upset and despite a deadline, you pause to sit with them.

▷ When you acknowledge your child's intuition and you're honest ('Yes, daddy and I are arguing right now. But you don't have to worry. We love each other, and we have the tools to work through it.').

▷ When your child is scared and you're not too quick to dismiss it.

▷ Seeing your child's negative moments as an opportunity for intimacy.

▷ Those three little words that we've come back to, as in multiple chapters: 'I believe you ...'

It can be a tough topic to think about as a parent, but it's important to be truthful with yourself. Do your children feel like they can trust you? This isn't about little white lies, like 'the park is closed today'. It's about putting marbles in their marble jar. The moments when they feel seen and heard; when they show or tell us that they feel vulnerable and we provide them with a safe haven.

In a podcast interview with Russel Brand on the topic of power, Brené Brown referenced a study undertaken in the 1950's. Two of the founders of American sociology, Barney G Glaser and Anselm L Strauss, set out to study the impact of 'death awareness' on adults and children who were dying. At the time, a lot of children were not told when their illnesses were terminal. Instead, they were told, everything is going to be okay. '[The researchers] wanted to better understand the impact this had on the children and if they believed it,' says Brené. 'So, they would sit down with the kids and say: tell me what's going on? What saturated across all the kids they talked to, is the kids said, 'I'm dying, but it must be really bad, and it must hurt a lot, because no one is telling me about it.'[3]

It matches up with the advice of many childhood cancer charities. We lie to our children to try and protect them from pain but we're ignoring their own instincts and powers of perception. Most children with advanced cancer already know that they are dying or think they might be. They know this from watching and listening to adults around them. They may also sense the changes in their bodies.[4]

Let's pull it back from cancer for a moment and apply it to the questions we've raised in earlier chapters:

▷ Are our children far wiser than we think they are?

▷ Within age-appropriate limits, how can we value their intuition?

▷ How is our own fear of time passing, impacting the way that we parent our children?

▷ If everything we face is a lesson in love, how could we talk to them with less fear?

▷ If we truly believe that we'll be together again, how do we want to build the foundation of this relationship (especially if this child could come back as your mother!)

Most importantly, how can we make sure that their marble jar of trust remains full (or, at least, never empty), so that when challenging events do happen in our lives, they can turn to us for a feeling of safety?

## ▷ Can We Trust Ourselves?

For me, a feeling of safety within a family comes down to one word: consistency. It's a word that I've had pinned on my mirror throughout my own motherhood. And, despite my best efforts, it's something that I can struggle with, especially during challenging periods for our family.

I want to consistently show up for my kids; to be consistently present, caring, loving and resilient. But a cocktail of past trauma and present struggles can make me veer from being Present Parent to being Distant Mother; one who hides in the toilet or tries to lose herself in Instagram. Unfortunately, when we feel overwhelmed or stressed it can be easy to detach—even from our own very-loved children. In the extreme it can have a long-term impact. In the psychological model of Attachment Theory, it's called a 'disorganised' attachment style—when a child experiences unpredictable and inconsistent behaviour from their caregiver in their formative years. Like most parents, this is the last thing that I would want for my own children.

What I've learned, through a lot of self-exploration and therapy, is that, in order to be consistent with my kids, I must learn to trust myself. To trust my resilience; to trust my capacity to love; to trust that I can be everything they need whilst continuing to be everything that I need for me. So, how do we get that kind of self-trust? It's a question you might have spent lifetimes asking ...

According to past life experts, previous events that we've experienced can cause a feeling of distrust in this life, or a lack of trust in our own minds and our own bodies. This can show up physically and emotionally, whether you struggle to have faith in your body's abilities or worry about your own mental wellness. It can even stop us from trusting our own happiness. Do you ever struggle to feel comfortable when life feels good? This could be because a past life has been so damn hard that any level of ease or satisfaction feels untrustworthy.

Stephanie Pesterfield is a past life and spiritual coach who posts on TikTok under The Celtic Brew. At the time of writing this book, Stephanie had just discovered that her 17-year-old son needed a lung transplant after being diagnosed with a rare autoimmune condition. Unable to make time for an interview, she was very happy for me to quote her TikTok videos and share her insight and knowledge. (Thank-you Stephanie and we're sending love to your son!) One of the common subjects that she explores is past life trauma and how it can impact how we parent in this lifetime. For example:

*You died from childbirth in a past life.*

▷ The most obvious sign is not wanting kids in this lifetime, out of a fear of childbirth.

▷ You might love children, but you refuse to have any biologically.

▷ If you have children, you have a debilitating fear that you or your child will die during childbirth (as a female it's normal to feel nervous about having a child, but this would be a debilitating fear. You can't stop thinking about it).

*You died young in a past life.*

▷ The most common sign is that you're afraid of dying young. You might even have an exact age in your mind that you think you're not going to live past.

▷ If you were a child, who died younger, you might have a fixation of children dying of your specific cause of death.

▷ Other people passing away in the same age-group that you were in when you died is going to be very triggering to you (everyone is upset when someone passes, but you might read a news story, and you can't stop thinking about it).

*You experienced past life sickness or plague.*

▷ You might be a serious germaphobe. You took COVID-19 way more seriously than others (and not for any reason explainable in your current lifetime).

▷ You're paranoid of any medical thing—you feared a pandemic before the pandemic happened.

▷ You have dreams or nightmares of being really sick.

▷ You might be someone who works in the medical field or has a healing gift.

As parents, we spend so much time being hard on ourselves. Even without the added complication of a past life, I know that I have a constant list of what-ifs in my head, many of which revolve around whether I will always be able to 'show up' for my family.

▷ Do you worry that you can't love your children because you didn't feel loved by your own parents?

▷ Do you worry that you won't be able to make enough money or support their future?

▷ Do you worry about your capacity to love?

▷ Do you worry about your capacity to watch them suffer as they grow?

▷ Do you worry about being happy enough, resilient enough, or any 'enough' for them?

*Welcome to parenthood ...*

How many of these worries would disappear if you could really trust your natural abilities to love and nurture; to heal and recover; to fulfill all your potential? For me, trust is about knowing that I have all the resources I need within me, whether my body is recovering from an injury, my heart is recovering from a breakup, or if I just need to endure another sleepless night with a teething baby. As they say: you've already survived 100 per cent of the hardest days in your life. Where's the evidence you can't keep going? Let's face it, parenting can feel like a slog! You don't always have to love it but do keep trusting that you were built for this.

On Stephanie's TikTok, someone asked the question: 'Is every past life as hard as this life?' Her answer was this: 'Not every lifetime is going to have the same level of difficulty.' In fact, that's why we might find ourselves drawn to a certain geographic location or time period. (Remember our Victorian England lover from an earlier chapter?) Perhaps, it's linked to one of your 'easier' past life periods.

This doesn't mean, we should dismiss or downplay any tougher time periods. 'It's important to remember that, most of the time, when we have difficult lives, they are lessons that our highest selves chose in some way,' says Stephanie. 'Now, that's not to say we chose every little thing or bad thing that has happened. But typically, we do know ahead of time that this lifetime is going to be a doozy. That's when we're going to learn life lessons the most. We don't learn and grow when life is easy.'

This is where it comes back to trust again. Trust in our capabilities. Trust in our child's abilities. Trust in our resilience within our soul family. Trust that we chose these experiences for a reason. Trust that we have free will and can decide how to react to a troubling situation. Trust that we are supported in every way.

As parents, we can build trust with our kids in the smallest and biggest ways. Last week, when my daughter lost her library bag for the third time, I told her, 'Even if you lose every possession you own, remember mummy will still love you.' And she knows that I will, because my behaviour displays it. Despite my fears that I'll be an 'inconsistent' mother, I always show up—like a fart smell you just can't shake. (To my little boy, that reference is for you!).

What I'm continuing to learn as a parent is, trust isn't about shielding people from hurt, it's about showing that, whatever happens, we'll be there for each other. A firm belief in the reliability of our bond and our capacity to adapt, and always find a source of happiness. And trust is a two-way street: you have to trust your kids, so they trust in you too.

## ▷ The Benefits of Belief

The concept of trust plays an important role for Anita and her family, which includes her husband, Bittu and their second child. 'I have always been spiritual, and I don't recall if I had more or less faith before [Milli's death],' says Anita. 'But, I do remember feeling trust that this was the right path for us all. Whenever people would say 'why us', we would say 'why not us?'. What makes us exempt from pain?'

Since Milli's death, Anita and her husband, Bittu, have gone on to create a beautiful skincare brand, Mauli Rituals, made with the healing power of Ayurvedic plant medicine and aromatherapy. In many ways, it was inspired by their past. Anita comes from a line of herbalists and her husband's father was an Ayurvedic doctor. During Milli's illness, Anita learnt the importance of taking care of yourself as a carer, including the benefits of soothing rituals.

'I don't know the master plan or why our soul's journey as they do, but I have a deep trust,' says Anita. 'Would I prefer she were here? Yes. Do I know that would be right for her? No. My trust has deepened with every passing year and my business also supports that faith and trust, as it teaches me daily.'

Throughout this book, I've promised that I wouldn't tell you what to believe—and I'm not going to start now. But it does appear that a belief in a 'masterplan' can help us to get through the toughest moments in life. As I've previously mentioned, research shows that spirituality and/or religion can help people cope with adversity by:

▷ encouraging them to reframe events through a hopeful lens,
▷ fostering a sense of connectedness; and
▷ cultivating connection through rituals[5].

If you've got this far into this book, I'm going to assume that you're not against the concept of rebirth—or at least you're considering that it could be a possibility. So, the next time that you're faced with a challenging situation, how could you fully trust that you were made for this? Or, to fall back on one of my favourite affirmations: 'I was created to cope with these circumstances.'

This doesn't mean that you'll be immune to worry. Anita admits that, when it comes to raising her son, Milli's death has, of course, had an impact. 'As his mother, I do feel concern over his wellbeing and the residue his life experience has left,' she says. 'But, this is his unique path and I believe we have all chosen this journey. He is a wonderful young man and if I look at it from a different lens, this experience has made him a deeply compassionate, kind, and loving soul.'

When Anita speaks about her experience of losing a child, what comes across is an astounding level of acceptance. She gives credit to the impact of her husband and her father-in-law. 'Through experience, one learns that resistance is futile,' adds Anita. 'My father-in-law had a saying, "do your best, leave the rest". Fear will not give us the energy to do our best, but acceptance does.'

During her grief, she has leant into the soothing power of reading and meditation to become 'much more aware of my thoughts and how they were hurting me and importantly, my relationships.' Like all of us, it's an ongoing process. 'I still feel fear, sometimes over the most trivial of things,' she says. 'But I now know how to be with it. We can all do that, and it lightens the load.'

## ▷ Changing Your Mental Fate

One in five new mums (and one in ten dads) experience postnatal anxiety or depression. I know that the topic of mental wellness is a worry for a lot of parents. Not only does it affect our own mental wellbeing, but can have a knock-on effect for our children. So, does mental illness follow us from lifetime to lifetime?

'The simple answer is no,' says Stephanie. 'Mental illness is on the earth plane not on the spiritual level. But, it is also very common for people to mirror the same cycle or the same people across lifetimes that might then lead to those mental health struggles.'

It can be frustrating when you're in the middle of a crisis and someone tells you, 'You can't change the situation, but you can change your reaction.' But this is relevant in this situation. Throughout multiple past lives, you could mirror a cycle of attracting lovers who don't value you; or trauma showing up as a physical symptom in your body. This could mean that, across multiple lifetimes, you experience anxiety or depression but—and this is the important but—it is the circumstances that you're repeating not your emotional reaction to it.

Why is this important? Because it can help us to feel more hopeful, especially if we've experienced mental health challenges in this lifetime. Just because you, or your children, have experienced depression or anxiety in this life, it doesn't mean it will be an eternal issue across future lifetimes. This is your permission slip to hope for the best in your next life (and this one), and that's important.

When I was pregnant with my third child, after experiencing Postnatal Depletion after my second child was born, it was my therapist who assured me: 'It can be different this time'. I needed someone to remind me that my mental fate wasn't set in stone. Nothing has to be forever.

The moral of this story? Mental illness isn't something that you carry forward, according to past life experts. But, it could be a repeated theme in your life if it's triggered by cyclic circumstances. You are not doomed to live a thousand anxious lives, just as you're not doomed to always be anxious in this lifetime. Even if you signed up to a journey that's a 'doozy', as Stephanie puts it, you can always choose how to respond (and think how good therapy could be by the year 2094!).

## Chapter 8 ▷ Thinking Points

▷ If our personality takes residue from past lives, how can we create more trust with our kids—for this lifetime and their future lifetimes?

▷ Can you think of three ways that you can add a marble to your kid's marble jar?

▷ Do you trust yourself? How can we expect our kids to trust us, if we don't trust our own emotional and physical capabilities?

▷ How would it feel to move through life deeply trusting that you are on the right path, including the moments which feel like suffering?

▷ This week, can you adopt the motto: 'do you best, leave the rest' and lighten your own mental load?

# Chapter 9:
## Tweens, Teens & Transitions

*Your child growing up is never just a loss; there is always something to gain.*

▷   When I was writing this book I was extremely aware that, at present, my kids are all less than seven years old with one of them still in the trenches of toddlerhood. Luckily, two of my past life advisors, who I leant on heavily when writing this book, are one step ahead of me in the parenting game—deep in the wild world of tweens and teenagers.

Although research shows that most children stop talking about their past lives by the age of seven, that doesn't mean that our young adults are outside this topic. In fact, you could say that our tween and teenage years are when our past life shadows really start to show up, and when a spiritual perspective is more important than ever. 'If you think about age, and what we subconsciously think about the youth and teenagers of today, we have a certain opinion,' says Justine Sharkie, who is now the parent of a growing tween.

When you think of the word teenager what words come into your mind? Difficult. Dramatic. Hormonal. Rebellious. Turbulent. Argumentative. As a parent, how does our perception of our kids ageing impact the way that we interact, emotionally and spiritually?

Justine recalls a past life regression experience with one of her one-on-one clients. This client remembered a past life in the city of Atlantis. You might have heard of the Lost City of Atlantis—in Ancient Greek Philosophy, it was said to be a utopian island that, one day, just vanished into the ocean (non-believers say that it never existed).

At the time, this client was going through a transition in her own life—moving from an adolescent energy to adulthood. According to Justine, in this soul timeline that she saw, she was the centre point of a ceremony. The ceremony was to celebrate her own initiation as an adolescent moving into 'the next stage of beingness'. 'She saw herself surrounded by people, older beings, wise-women crone energy, and younger, infant energies,' explains Justine. 'These women were coming to witness her evolution from teenager into adulthood. They all came to witness her new level of awakening; her new level of embodiment.'

When the past life session ended, the memory had a long-lasting, positive impact on Justine, as well as her client. 'What stuck with me was, they came, not only with joy for her, but because they wanted to witness creation itself,' adds Justine. 'When I had that experience through my client, I realised how much we, without realising it, judge ourselves for our next evolution. I work with a lot of clients who can feel the next evolution coming through them but they're so fearful of what people will think of them. We're so conditioned to not ever feel safe to evolve. We feel this energy of creation in our soul wanting to move through us, but we try to hold it in.'

When I heard this story, it hit me deeply. I was the so-called 'difficult' teenager who felt judged for self-exploration, including my friendship choices, my career choices, and my sexual experiences. At times in my life, I also felt like I had to hold myself back and 'stay a child' so that people around me would feel more comfortable.

(I think, this was a secondary thread in my eating disorder—the desire to keep my body as small and 'innocent' as possible.)

If we had a 'difficult' teenage transition (in this life or a past life), it can deeply impact our fear of our children ageing—and society doesn't make it any easier. If you've got children, have you already been warned, 'you wait until they become a teenager ... you won't know what's hit you.' We're told to dread our kid's teenage years before they're even out of nappies. We're told, they'll ignore us or hate us. We're warned that, when they fly the nest, we'll feel hopeless and purposeless. No wonder, their evolution can feel like a threat to our very being.

For Justine, this is why her client's past life experience was so impactful. She compares her client's memory of the coming-of-age ceremony to the fairy movie, *Tinker Bell*. 'I don't know if you've seen Tinker Bell the movie where she emerges and has to find her gift,' she says. 'All the other fairies come and go: who is she going to be? There's no jealousy and no 'I want her to be like this ...' There's a joy of witnessing the emergence of this potential.'

If we believe in the old hierarchy of parenting, that adults have all the answers and children don't know anything, then our children growing up can feel like a threat because it rocks that boat. In a mindset of scarcity, it feels like our children growing up must mean that we're losing something (our youth, our control, our own wisdom). But, what if you looked at it in another way?

As your children grow into their wisdom, we get to go along for the ride, to learn from them and grow with them. Think of it this way: if life is cyclical, you are going to be a tween and teenager again once day. How would you like to be celebrated as you transition through the ages? How can you put aside your own fears to celebrate your child's 'next stage of beingness'?

## ▷ Rites of Passage

'What isn't made sacred is made shameful.' I first heard this phrase during a workshop with the matrescence expert Amy Taylor Kabbaz and, ever since then, it has stuck with me. The facilitator was talking about our teenage rites of passage—getting our first period, losing our virginity, leaving home for the first time, or experiencing our first heartbreak. With all these milestones, 'what isn't made sacred is made shameful'. Unfortunately, in the Western world, we often forfeit the first and lean into the second.

Despite thinking that society has come 'so far', we are still awkward and backwards when it comes to matters of the body. One study, which was only conducted three years ago, found that a third of parents feel awkward talking about periods to their children.[1] When it comes to sex, 20 per cent of parents don't have 'the talk' at all with their kids, like, ever (and, parents, I know it's hard and they've already learnt everything from TikTok!). Of the parents who did, one in four said it was 'awkward.'[2] Even in our supposed sex-positive culture, there is still a lot of shame around sexuality. I get it—it comes from a place of fear. As parents, we don't want to put our children in dangerous sexual situations.

The problem is that as soon as we make something shameful, we shut down all conversations. And, in doing so, we don't learn about the different shades of experiences that our children, tweens and teens are having. When it comes to every rite of passage there isn't only one cookie cutter way to experience it.

▷ You don't just 'lose your virginity' in one way—especially when the idea of virginity is a social construct in the first place. (Don't get me started on that topic!).

▷ You don't just get your first period in one way.

▷ You don't just leave home in one way.

▷ You don't just experience heartbreak in one way.

Generations of parents before us were told to 'just have the talk'. One talk. Box tick for sex education. But, more than ever, we can't just have a 'one and done' approach to these discussions, whether it's our bodies changing, our first sexual experiences, or any of the firsts that we experience in tweens and adolescents. All of these firsts are spiritual experiences.

When I was about 10 years old, I saw a female family friend buying what I now know was a box of sanitary products. When I asked what they were, I can't remember exactly what she told me. But, it was a short explanation with no time for questions. For the next two years, I was utterly terrified of seeing blood in the toilet, because I thought that it was a sign that I was dying. Every time I'd go to the bathroom, I remember, I'd stare into the toilet bowl. As a little girl it consumed me, until I became more educated about my own body. By the time I got my period I didn't worry about it at all ... but there was another layer to my story.

As I shared in my last book, *The World is a Nice Place*, I danced with an eating disorder for years from the age of 16. The turning point for me was a session with my spiritual healer in London. During our time together, I uncovered a past life when I died by drinking contaminated water from a river (leaving me with a fear of consuming anything that wasn't 'safe' or felt like a threat to me).

During that healing session, I also learnt that my death occurred soon after I had started my period. At the time, in that life, I had fallen in love, but my parents disapproved of the boy that I had fallen in love with. They had warned me that after I 'became a woman' I would be expected to marry someone else—a better match for me. Now I suspect that I drank the contaminated water out of choice because I didn't want to be pushed into a marriage.

In hindsight, it feels as though a fear around my menstrual cycle has shown up in different ways for me throughout different lifetimes. In this life, when my first husband died, I didn't have a period for seven years. (My last bleed was on the day of his funeral.) After trying multiple medical methods to get it back I had all but given up. Then, out of nowhere, it suddenly returned ... the week after I met my now-husband. I learnt in another past life session, the boy I was in love with when I died from drinking contaminated water is my current life partner. When we met again, my soul exhaled, and my period returned.

Interestingly, when I was writing about this, I had another personal aha moment. When my second son was born, when my water broke, it was the colour of blood. I went on to have a very healthy and natural birth. But afterwards I felt traumatised. I couldn't shake the feeling of looking down, seeing blood and feeling totally out of control. Could it all be linked? When I listened to my intuition, the answer felt like: yes. (I'll talk more about how I've started to 'repattern' these fears in the chapter, *Shameless Parenting.)*

This is a convoluted way to say that we are complex souls. The way that your child reacts to growing up—and the way you react to them growing up—cannot be compared to their peers, or a black-and-white process taken from a book about adolescence. To support our teens and tweens, how can we become more aware of their big picture, including their potential past life experiences—the people they are growing up to be, and the people they have been in the past?

## ▷ Open Conversations

Unlike our kids, who seem all too happy to chat about their past lives, getting our teens to go there could be more difficult. Studies show that spirituality does dip in our teenage years, although it's not universal[3]. In fact, research has identified two group differences in adolescence. In the teenage years, belief and participation in religious activity can decline. Or, young people tend to engage in spiritual exploration that has enduring implications throughout their life.

A research paper from a team at Deakin University explored 'expressions of spirituality' in Australian teens. A study cited in that paper concluded, 22 per cent reported being 'spiritual but not religious' and 16 per cent 'religion and spiritual' — and total of 38 per cent. It also reports, 50 per cent of them believe in karma, 29 per cent in reincarnation and 20 per cent in astrology. Significant numbers of Australian teens also reported experiencing an awareness of a higher presence or power (58 per cent) or a connection to nature (76 per cent) on at least one occasion.

The psychologist, Doctor Lisa Miller, author of *The Spiritual Child,* has spent years researching the impact of spirituality on children and adolescents. In her book, she says that spirituality runs through our life in two threads:

  ▷ *Transcendent awareness.* Our hard-wired capacity to see into the deeper nature of life; to know that we are loved, held, guided and never alone.
  ▷ *For that to be shared with each other.* So that we can show up and be part of the symphony of life, where we are loved, held, guided and never alone.

I am incredibly grateful that my parents taught me to meditate when I was in my late teens. Despite the fact that I had stopped going to church years earlier, when I went to university, I stuck a crucifix on my wall which I would talk to every night, next to a photo of my dad who, at that point, was bald from a period of intensive chemotherapy. I always say of my kids, 'I don't care what they believe in ... but I do want them to believe in something.'

When my daughter came home talking about Jesus dying on the cross, I was okay with it. (If she begins talking about hell, I might have to gently question it.)

Saying this, I have been very clear with my kids that nobody knows exactly what happens when we die. We get to believe what we choose to believe and so does everyone around us. Last week, my little boy came home from day-care and said, 'You know how, when you die, you become a star in the sky and then you can choose to come back? One of the boys in my class said that isn't true.' Initially, I brushed him off (forgive me, I was making dinner!). The next day, when we were hiking, I circled back to the conversation because I knew I hadn't completed the cycle:

*'Remember what you told me about that little boy in your class? The truth is, nobody knows exactly what happens when we die. We get to choose what we believe. I choose to believe, we can come back and be a baby again because of certain things I've heard and experienced. Nobody knows for sure. It's the reason, dying is such an exciting adventure because we get to solve the mystery.'*

We are lucky to live close to one of the largest Buddhist temples in the Southern Hemisphere called Nan Tien Temple; a two hours' drive south of Sydney. My kids were all blessed there and frequently visit, pausing to light incense at the entrance to the main temple and to ring the 'gratitude bell'. I don't go out of my way to school them on Buddhism, but I do believe in the power of immersion—spending time in spaces and places where people consider that they are more than just their physical bodies. I want them to know, we are more than just a meat-suit.

What might surprise you is that a survey of teens across eight countries found that a lot of adolescents want to talk about spirituality more. 'In regard to young people, the assumption tends to be that they need to be taught what to believe (they are 'empty vessels') or that they are not very interested,' wrote the researchers. 'As a result, it appears that young people in many different parts of the world do not have many opportunities to talk about or examine this area of life.'

In the eight-country survey, they found that about one-third of youth surveyed said they talked at least monthly with their friends about spiritual issues such as the meaning of life, what is faith, and why we are on Earth? In the focus groups, most young people welcomed the opportunity to explore the subject with intention and purpose, and without any fear of being judged as wrong.[4]

When it comes to discussing spirituality, the Centre for Spiritual Development in Childhood and Adolescence has this advice for parents:

  ▷ Do not be afraid to discuss spiritual questions, even if you don't have all the answers.
  ▷ Listen to and respect what your teen has to say, even if you do not completely agree.
  ▷ Be a good role model of your own spiritual beliefs, practices, and commitments.
  ▷ Nurture your children's gifts and talents by allowing them to express their spirituality through journals, music, art, etc.
  ▷ Help your teen connect with spiritual leaders and mentors, other than yourself.
  ▷ Encourage your teens to surround themselves with positive friends who strengthen their spiritual growth[5].

Of course, this can feel easier said than done. As my friends who have tweens and teenagers constantly tell me, it's not always easy to impart knowledge on that age group. If it does feel like you're hitting your head against the brick wall, just remind yourself: there is plenty of time to find yourself, spiritually. In fact, 'spiritual maturity' is a constant evolution, which continues over your lifespan.

It may not look like visiting a church or setting up an alter in your bedroom. It could simply be immersing yourself in a green scene. 'Eco-spirituality' is an approach to faith that celebrates humanity's connection to the natural world. And, for teenagers, it can provide a solution to 'eco-anxiety'. If you want to connect with your teen, it could be time to 'rewild' your spirituality—go for a hike in the forest, take up rock climbing or surfing. Immerse yourselves in nature, together. See if it promotes a sense of 'oneness', not only within your family, but with the universe.

## ▷ Teens' Changing Worlds

Whilst I was writing this chapter, Justine sent me a voice message, after she had a very revealing conversation with her tweenaged daughter. (This story is shared with her daughter's permission.) As I mentioned earlier, Justine and her daughter both experience triggers around food. For both of them, this shows up in different ways.

*Food is safety.* For Justine, it shows up as an addiction to food. 'I cannot leave the house without grabbing something and putting it in my mouth,' she says. 'I can't go to school pick-up or even head out for a little walk. The times I've tried, my body physically won't let me.'

*Food is fear.* For her daughter, it has shown up in an aversion to food. 'She seems to hate food,' says Justine. 'It's like she's had a fear of food since she was a baby.

She doesn't like to eat; she only eats very plain food. It's such a stress in our family.'

For a while, Justine has suspected they share a past life experience, which is showing up in different ways for both of them. For Justine, she needs food to feel safe. For her daughter, it's quite the opposite. The night before I wrote this chapter, she decided to, lightly, broach the subject with her daughter. This is how Justine brought it up:

*'Do you believe in past lives?'*

*'I've got a theory ... You know how you and I have very different food things. Do you reckon it's possible we had a past life together and something traumatic happened, which is putting a lot of stress around food in this lifetime?'*

In Justine's house this isn't an unusual conversation. Her kids are used to discussing cosmic matters but this was the first time she'd addressed their eating issues directly. How did her daughter respond? 'She paused the telly, which doesn't happen in our house,' says Justine. 'She said to me, "Maybe we ate something that was really poisonous, or something really contaminated."'

When Justine didn't respond instantly, her daughter kept talking—for half an hour. She revealed to her mum that, three times a year, she has the same dream: 'There is a woman underwater. She has a flowing dress and she's calling my name. She's yelling at me. It sounds really angry but it's actually loving and kind. She's trying to tell me, I'm here to do something very important.'

She then told Justine her theory: 'I believe there are all these worlds happening at the same time. They're all connected so one world impacts the other world. And I'm going to do something in this world that saves another world.'

Out of the mouth of a ten-year-old, there's an explanation for past life and quantum entanglement in a nutshell. And, although the conversation didn't give an instant fix to their eating issues, Justine says, it offered a way to move forward (and not everything needs a quick-fix solution).

'It now feels like we can work on it together and it's a way we can work through our food trauma,' she says. 'Even today, I was eating, but I knew I wasn't hungry. It was just my old patterning coming up. I knew I was doing it, but I told myself that it was okay. One day, I'll have the consciousness to move through this.'

Since then, she has begun exploring Emotional Freedom Technique (EFT) with the help of an EFT coach, and has also begun sharing the techniques with her daughter. When she worries about her tween, she comes back to the revelation that her daughter shared with her that day: 'I'm going to do something in this world that saves another world.'

Whilst I don't want my kids to feel the pressure to save the world (or worlds!), I do want them to feel connected to something bigger than themselves. And to know, they are incredibly powerful. Their inner compass can lead the rest of the way.

## Chapter 9 ▷ Thinking Points

▷ Think about your own adolescence and the words used to describe you. Are these old narratives having an impact on how you parent your growing children?

▷ Think back to your rites of passage, including starting your period or losing your virginity. Were they made sacred or shameful?

▷ How could you support open conversations in your home that promote a feeling of 'oneness' with the university rather than otherness?

▷ Have fun with eco-spirituality. Plan an outing with your teen or tween that connects you with nature and, as a side-effect, with each other.

▷ Ask your teen the question: what does spirituality mean to you and your friends? You might be surprised by their answer.

# Chapter 10:
# Standing Out & Fitting In

*Finally, let's end our tireless quest for normal.*

▷ If you're reading this book, I suspect that your child—or multiple children—was born with a part of their being that surprised you. Perhaps you had one 'easy' child who read like a parenting handbook. Then number two or three came along, and suddenly you went from feeling like a parenting expert to a total failure.

Even if you are trying to parent against the paradigm, we can all find ourselves thinking, 'I just want my child to fit in.' We want them to be 'popular', especially if we were not. We measure their milestones against their peers from infanthood, comparing the age they slept through the night, whether they're potty-trained or eating solids.

As they get older, we're overly aware of their grades and whether they're 'keeping up' with their classmates. Our need to fit in–or stand out in a superior way—can be overheard in conversations at the school gates or the bus stop. Even if we profess that we're happy for our child to stand out, do we really believe it? Or, would we really prefer our kids to fit in? Because, on a primitive level, fitting in isn't a threat. And we all want to save our kids from perceived danger.

The truth is, our children want to fit in too. In fact, research has found that our desire to fit in starts around the age of three. According to one study by Duke University Researchers, this is the age in which children start to go along with what others say or do, even if it overrides their own personal preferences[1]. In fact, finding a way to fit in is an important part of childhood development—it gives our kids a feeling of safety and security. But, is there a way that we can give our kids a sense of belonging without making them feel afraid of their differences?

And, in a culture that loves labels, can we allow ourselves to really see our children rather than pathologise them?

## ▷ New Age Neurodiversity

Thanks to a growing awareness around neurodiversity, our kids and their kids will, hopefully, grow up in a world where the natural difference in people's brains is seen as a strength and not a weakness. According to the Royal Children's Hospital, it is estimated that one in 20 children in Australia have attention deficit hyperactivity disorder (ADHD), and it is more prevalent in boys than girls. (Though this could be because girls are better at masking the symptoms.)

I have multiple mum friends who have just received an ADHD diagnosis for their children; many of these mums have also been diagnosed themselves during the process. I know, from them, that it can come with some grief and fears for their child's future. That's why I'm here to offer an important reframe.

When I look around my ADHD mum friends, I can clearly see a common thread: they're incredibly spiritual and connective; they work as psychics and mediums; they're the people I gravitate towards for advice, guidance and healing.

Within the spiritual community, I've heard a different meaning for the acronym ADHD: Access Directly (to) Higher Dimensions. Are children with ADHD more spiritually 'in-tune' than other children? The past life experts that I interviewed seem to think so.

Peter Smith, the founder of the Institute for Quantum Consciousness supports the work of past life researchers like Mary Rodwell who write about 'star seeds'—the name for souls who have reincarnated from 'off planet'. Instead of a soul reincarnating from earth, the theory is that they've come from somewhere else in the universe. 'A lot of these kids don't do what other kids do', says Peter. 'They're energetically sensitive. They're rebelling in the school system. They're put down as 'bad kids' with ADHD. I've had this conversation with a lot of people—ADHD is just the rewiring of the human form to get ready for the next frequencies coming through.'

According to Peter, if someone is more 'cosmic' in their soul lineage, they are potentially more energetically sensitive, especially to other people's emotions and external stimuli. 'They are probably used to being part of a group consciousness,' he explains. 'We have this unique separate consciousness as humans on this planet, but that's not the norm.' He has worked with clients who can remember being 'consciously entangled' with 10 or 11 people in a previous life based on a different planet. 'Connected consciousness is something that is a phenomenon across the universe, but we don't get it here very well,' adds Peter.

In his experience, starseed children can be very close to their mothers, but this connection is a great thing. In his healing work, he often works with mothers as 'substitutes' for their children, because the link is so strong the healing can have a ripple effect. In fact, he says mothers can consciously ripple health and happiness to their children, and you don't need a past life expert to help you do it. 'If you do a health cleanse and you feel better, like you're in a higher frequency, you can share that with your child,' adds Peter. 'You can deliberately ripple it to them.'

To be honest, I was in two minds as to whether to include the topic of offplanet rebirth in this book, especially in a chapter on new age neurodiversity. But, to me, it's not about labelling children as 'extra-terrestrial'. It's about realising that every human on this planet is different and the sooner we stop comparing ourselves, the better.

As a parent of a neurodivergent child, it's also about realising, you are the perfect parent to raise them. Research shows, ADHD tends to run in families, and, in most cases, it's thought the genes you inherit from your parents are a significant factor in developing the condition. So, it's likely, either you or your partner are neurodivergent. This means, you probably also have 'access directly to higher dimensions'. Do you feel it? How can you use it to your advantage?

Recently, one of my mum friends was diagnosed with ADHD. She had pursued a diagnosis after her 13-year-old daughter was diagnosed with the condition. After an initial period of grieving, she sees it as a blessing that she gets to explore the diagnosis alongside her teenager. 'I remind myself, I'm the perfect parent for her,' she says. 'How could the cosmos put a mother and a baby together, on a soul level, that aren't made to go together. We are the lock and the key for each other.'

## ▷ A Parenting Privilege

When I was writing this chapter, I called on my good friend, Jane, whose teenage son, Tahi, was diagnosed with Autism Spectrum Disorder (ASD) as a toddler. For the last seven years she has also worked in the education sector, supporting children with ADHD and autism. It was her son who convinced her that past lives are real. During a conversation about childhood memories, Tahi came out with a recollection, 'I remember being in your tummy. And I remember before I came here.' When Jane asked what it was like, he replied, 'It was really nice, quiet and dark. But, I wasn't scared. I was just floating around there.'

At the time of our conversation, Jane had just returned from a school camp for children living with disability. In her group there were multiple children with severe autism. One little boy, who we'll call Adam, is 11 years old and non-verbal. But he and Jane's son can communicate perfectly, using hand gestures, which they created and only they can understand. From a young age Tahi has been able to communicate with non-verbal children with no barrier. At the age of five, he formed his first non-verbal friendship. As he explained to Jane, 'I don't need to hear words, mummy. I know what he's thinking.'

It's just one of many examples Jane has experienced of neurodivergent children seeing each other, and the world, in a unique and amazing way. One of the attendees of the school camp was born with muscular dystrophy and, therefore, uses a wheelchair. 'Another little boy who has severe autism came up to us looking worried,' recalls Jane. 'He said, "I'm worried that he can't walk ... I've got an idea." He went away, got a pair of scissors, came back and said, "You can take my bone. Then he can walk. I want him to have my bones."'

When she talks about the children she works with, Jane lights up. 'It's beautiful to watch,' she says. 'People say that children on the autism spectrum don't have empathy, but you should see them. I get paid to be with them, but I'd do it for free. It's such a privilege.' As Jane explains, a lot of children with ASD walk on their toes. This is thought to be caused by a dysfunctional vestibular system, a common problem in autism. Jane has another theory: 'I think it's because they don't always want to be here. They know there's somewhere else to be.'

## ▷ Gender and Sexuality

More recently, The University of Virginia has worked on research in the area of childhood gender nonconformity and childhood past life memories.[2] In a study of 469 children, they found that 'children who remembered a life involving a different natal sex were much more likely to exhibit gender nonconformity than children who remembered a same sex life.'

In other words, if a child remembers a past life as a woman but, in this life, they are assigned male at birth, they are more likely to identify as the sex they have reported to be previously. The study concluded that, 'Among children who report memories of a previous life, gender nonconformity is strongly associated with a purported life as a member of a different sex.'

I'm going to keep this section of the book brief, because this topic is extremely complex, but important. In our household, I have talked about the fluidity of gender with my kids from a very young age, and it's a topic that comes up naturally in conversation surprisingly frequently. This research, into a possible link between past lives and gender nonconformity, is an interesting new perspective. I'm intrigued to see how it develops.

So, what about sexuality and reincarnation? It's a relationship explored by the late Louise Hay, the founder of Hay House, who began supporting men with HIV in the nineties. (In her bestselling books, she stopped capitalising the acronym 'hiv' because she didn't want to give it so much power.) According to Louise, the soul has 'no sexuality'. But, at the start of every life, we decide what sexuality to practice during our next lifetime, depending on the patterns we want to work through.

In a message to the LGBTQIA+ community, Louise wrote:

'Each lifetime I seem to choose a different sexuality. Sometimes I am a man, sometimes I am a woman. Sometimes I am heterosexual, sometimes I am homosexual. Each form of sexuality has its own areas of fulfillment and challenges. Sometimes society approves of my sexuality and sometimes it does not. Yet at all times, I am me—perfect, whole, and complete.'

As with all matters of self-love and acceptance, we can't fully teach it to our kids until we practise it with ourselves. Dig deep, parents. Explore your own sexual shame and gender rigidities. How can you role model safe, sexual expression for your children (in an age-appropriate way, of course). How can you play with gender roles in your own home? If you've lived, and loved, as different genders across different lifetimes, how can you loosen your hold on the binary?

Personally, this is one of the reasons I love my husband. He wears eyeliner to my kid's birthday party. He is the parent who dyes my daughter's hair pink and blue. He is an adrenaline-loving adventurer ... and he wears a sarong with his work boots when he's chopping wood in the garden. My kids don't blink, because this is their normal.

As Louise wrote: 'This is a time for healing, for making whole, not for condemnation. We must rise out of the limitations of the past. We are all divine, magnificent expressions of life.'

## How to Feel Safe to Stand-Out

*An exercise from Justine Sharkie*

▷ Take a deep breath.

▷ Repeat this mantra over and over while being super present with your energy body: *'It is safe for me to not be understood by others.'*

▷ Notice what sensations, feelings and thoughts that come up when you say these words. Hopefully it's heavy, sticky and somewhat painful, because then you'll know you're getting to your deep subconscious.

▷ While you repeat the words, tap gently under your collar bones (your 'high heart'). This sends calming signals to your nervous system and amygdala.

▷ Rinse and repeat until you feel confident, light, playful and grateful for your uniqueness.

## Chapter 10 ▷ Thinking Points

▷ How many of your struggles as a parent stem from a need to fit in or a deep desire to be seen as 'normal'?

▷ How could you pause, really 'see' your child during challenging situations, and tap into your intuition to soothe them?

▷ Could neurodiversity be a sign of spiritual connection? If your child isn't neurotypical, do they seem to have a deeper wisdom or inner knowing?

▷ If a family could be said to share a collective consciousness, how could you use this to your advantage to cultivate calmness and harmony?

# PART 3: REPARENTING YOURSELF

*Our words have the power to change our own lives. Now, this might sound minor compared to changing the world, but it's huge.*

*Everything we do comes from within, and the messages we give ourselves shape who we are and how we interact with the world. Our inner voice impacts our wellbeing, guides our moral compass and fuels our actions.*

*We must start by valuing ourselves so we can value others— by telling ourselves messages that positively impact our mental health and self-worth. When we make a mistake, instead of asking ourselves 'What is wrong with me?', we can simply think, 'How could I do better?'*

*Our inner voice is the most powerful voice we hear—we must use it wisely.*

Lucian, aged 12

# Chapter 11:
# Healing Timelines

*Healing can come in the most unlikely moments.*

▷ Now that we're over halfway through this book, I feel like I can get a bit out-there with you (as if off-planet reincarnation wasn't out-there enough!) and start to share the areas of my book research that surprised me the most and were also the most impactful to me personally. One memorable moment came during an 'ancestral activation', which ended in a ceremony where I pulled my ancestor's 'energetic blueprint' out of my body. More specifically, I pulled it out of my vagina like a placenta! Don't worry, I am going to explain it further. But, first of all, let's go back to the concept of ancestral healing which led me to this ceremony in the first place.

In a previous chapter, we talked about how parents are 'consciously entangled' with their children. This means that, if we do the work to heal ourselves, we can also ripple that healing to our offspring. According to past life experts it can also work backwards. Could healing ourselves also heal the generations that came before us, even if they're no longer with us? And could healing our ancestor's pains also heal us and, as a knock-off effect, heal our children?

This is an idea that Justine Sharkie shares in her course, *Five days of Visibility Healing*. There are four different paradigms of soul work, according to Justine—the places you can go on your timeline to begin to access healing. These are:

▷ your human experience in this life
▷ your past lifetimes
▷ your ancestral lineage; and
▷ your soul's journey in places other than the earth.

We've covered points one and two in earlier chapters: how you can explore your current day triggers and past life bruises to release trauma. It was the third one, your ancestral lineage, that caught my attention. The idea is that the energy of our ancestors can become encoded in our own energy. This can include different shadows that people of your bloodline have held within them. As you'll remember, a shadow is anything which stops us from remembering our true selves and trusting our intuition.

Shadows can show up as physical ailments, our belief systems, emotions that we experience or suppress, or blockages in our spiritual energy or intuition. Of course, these aren't all shadows inherited from our ancestors ... but they could be. And there is a way to 'gift it back' to them. 'This idea can feel heavy, like you're doomed, but it's a gift,' says Justine. 'Once you heal energy through your ancestral timelines, you open so much energy for yourself. It moves into the web of light we're connected to.'

She uses the word 'surrogating'. (Verb: to put in the place of another, to appoint a successor, deputy, or substitute for oneself.) Is it possible that when your ancestors left their last lifetime, they passed on their shadows for you to surrogate? More specifically, did you actively choose to surrogate a shadow for them, with the goal that you would clear it on their behalf? If yes, have you managed it? And how can you prevent passing it onto your own children?

## ▷ **Your Soul Inheritance**

If you were born into a minority group, the idea of a 'Soul Inheritance' might not feel new to you. In Australia, for example, the offspring of the Stolen Generation may feel, decades after the crime, the impact of the fear felt by their ancestors. The cultural trauma experienced by African Americans over more than 300 years of their enslavement has in many cases been transmitted to the current generation.

Even if you don't belong to a marginalised group, have you ever thought about your own Soul Inheritance? The 'soul assets' that an individual bequeaths to their loved ones after they pass away; assets that, according to past life theory, you agreed to as per your Soul Contract. Most of us have heard stories about our grandparents, great-grandparents, and their parents before them. Do you ever notice any patterns, common threads, or similarities?

▷ Has anyone ever said to you, 'All the women in this family are ...?'

▷ Does everyone share an illness or physical characteristic?

▷ Do you have eerily similar life experiences to an ancestor (for example, my great grandma and I were both widowed at 23 years old)?

▷ Do you feel like you inherited guilt, shame, fear, or embarrassment around a certain aspect of life or yourself, which seems to have been with you since birth?

▷ Have you ever heard your family described as 'cursed' or unlucky?

... These could all be a clue to your soul inheritance.

If you've inherited a shadow, it's unlikely to just be you. It's likely that one of your parents and their parents also carried it before you—and perhaps continue to carry it alongside you. When it comes to shadow healing, Justine has four main principles: be curious, be compassionate, be committed, and love the shit out of yourself during the process. She believes that shadow work has a bad reputation as always being heavy and painful. But, there are ways to explore your shadow with amazement and even pleasure.

I was certainly amazed during the fourth day of her visibility healing course. The goal of the course is to explore shadows that impact our self-belief and self-confidence, so we can feel safe to be who we truly are. On the fourth day, we moved into healing our ancestral shadows. (See the Appendix for how to access this course). At the start of the activation, Justine explained:

*'We have the power and responsibility because we are the ones here in physical form. We have the power to heal so much of our ancestor's soul experience—to heal their light body. They're unable to do it now wherever they've gone on their soul's journey. It needs to be done in the physical world. We are their champions, their ambassadors, the alchemists who hold this power in the physical form. Through healing them, it opens so much of ourselves up, because it takes so much energy to hold a lot of dense energy and negative patterns from our ancestral lineage.'*

During the activation, which felt like a deep meditation, I was guided through a 'portal', led by one of my parents and one of my grandparents. Then, through a 50-minute process, I was led to identify the energetic 'blueprint' that I was surrogating for one of my ancestors. Straight away, two words came into my mind: sexual shame. I had a vision of one of my ancestors—a woman that I didn't recognise—and my own grandmother. This shame wasn't new to the women in my family; it ran like a thread through multiple generations.

I almost laughed when I thought about my experiences in this lifetime. After my first husband died when I was 23 years old, I dealt with my grief by sleeping around. I then wrote a book, *Wife Interrupted*, about my promiscuity. When that book came out, I received a lot of backlash, especially from people in Ireland where my late husband was born. This was over ten years ago when slut-shaming was still rampant, especially in certain religious communities. And here I was, 15 years later, unlocking the sexual shame of my ancestors. It felt like a full-circle moment.

During the final section of the meditation, I was invited to take part in a 'regifting' ceremony. During this ceremony I was given a choice: I could continue to carry this blueprint with me, or I could give it back to my ancestors. As Justine explained, I wasn't just giving it back: 'You're gifting it back and they're receiving it better.'

For years, I'd been adjusting and adapting the blueprint; doing the work to heal previous generations. Every sexual encounter I'd had in this lifetime; every yes and every no; every time I'd spoken my truth, knowing that I'd be criticised, was part of my work to shift the shadow which I was surrogating for generations.

I'll never forget the moment that I released the blueprint from my 'internal energy body'. In my mind, the sexual shame looked and felt like slime—the homemade kind that my kids love. It was stuck to the inside of my skin, throughout my entire body. With Justine's guidance, I imagined the slime loosening and detaching, until I could pull it out of my body. And what better exit than out of my vagina?

As I visualised releasing the blueprint with both hands, it felt ... liberating. If you've ever birthed a baby vaginally (without trauma), the best way I can describe it is, the moment that you birth your placenta. The relief, the amazement, the lightness, the freedom the struggle is over.

When I imagined handing the blueprint back to my ancestor, I understood. They could have never worked through this sexual shame in their lifetime; in the society, country, and culture they were born into. Only I could do the work that I have done; in the nineties and noughties, as a woman of privilege in the country that I was born in. And it's still been bloody hard at times, even for me!

Interestingly, this wasn't the last time the topic of sex came up in my past life exploration. In our chapter on *Shameless Parenting*, I'll share the 'repatterning' process, which led to a huge leap in my personal healing, and why our past lives lived as nuns, sex workers and martyrs can lead to our shadows. For now, take a few moments to think:

▷ What blueprint could you be surrogating within yourself?

▷ What are you healing for your ancestors?

▷ Do you still have work to do, or is that blueprint no longer serving you?

▷ How would it feel to gift it back to them—better than you received it?

Most importantly, is it time you gave back that blueprint, so that you don't pass it onto your own babies? Isn't that why we do the work after all? It's probably a large part of why you're reading this book in the first place ...

## ▷ The Forward Motion of Ancestral Forgiveness

When I was writing this chapter, one of my friends sent me an episode of the podcast *The Spiritually Sassy Show*. The host, Sah D'Simone was talking to teacher, healer, author, musician and ecologist Vir McCoy.[1] The topic was: 'Feeling the Feelings My Ancestors Never Felt'. (I highly recommend listening to the whole podcast episode).

Through his own experiences of healing Lyme Disease and, later, recovering from long COVID, Vir has explored 'the power of making peace with our lineage's past'. In his opinion, a lot of the trauma that we experience in this life is 'unfelt feelings', whether it's from our own childhood or even the unfelt feelings of our ancestors.

'There is this level,' says Vir. 'Great grandpa did some shitty things or experienced some trauma they just couldn't deal with. Grandpa died with this in him. Dad couldn't heal it. Here we are, these sensitive beings, and we have got to deal with it now.' To do this, he spent 10 days in meditation in the desert, but the good news is, you don't have to go to that extreme.

According to Vir, the first step of the healing journey is dropping into these unresolved, undigested emotions, whilst recognising they are not yours to carry. As he puts it: 'Feel all the feelings that never got felt, even if they aren't yours. But, don't attach to them because that is not who you are.'

Take a few moments to think back on your ancestral history and the unfelt feelings that you may have inherited. An obvious place to start is your elders who were living, and even served, in the two World Wars. If your great-grandfather fought in a war, what horrors did he seem or take part in? If your great-grandmother had a 'war child' out of wedlock, like mine did, did she ever process the shame of being sent away to birth them? If your grandparent was orphaned in the War, how did they process their grief abandonment. (Let's remember, therapy was not normalised back then.)

Now, how can you make a 'living amends' for your ancestors? How can you live, and love, in a way that heals their old hurts and remedies their fears from the past?

It reminds me of an essay by the poet Ross Gay, the author of *The Book of Delights*. Every day for a year, he wrote an essay about something that delighted him to remind him of the purpose and pleasure of celebrating everyday wonders. On his 42nd birthday, as he was getting dressed, Ross decided to go for floral everything. Floral socks. Floral earrings. Even floral underwear. In doing so, he sent healing back to his father, who was raised in less progressive times.

'It's a little bit of healing for my old man,' he writes. 'Surely he would warn us against wearing red, lest we become to some stereotype I barely even know. A delight that we can heal our loved ones, even the dead ones.'

Ancestral healing can happen in gentle and subtle ways. When you're meditating, imagine that you're sitting at the centre of a web of light with generations of ancestors linked together on all sides of you. When you're playing with your kids in the garden or squashed in a bathtub as a family, take a few moments to imagine your ancestors watching over you, smiling.

Here's the twist: you don't have to change yourself to make them happy. By living out loud, as yourself, trust that you are playing your part in all your soul contracts. Over the years, I've carried shame about how outspoken I've been about sex and self-pleasure, imagining the reaction of my Irish-Catholic grandparents. But it was part of my role to shake up the barrel. My own children will continue it, hopefully with less resistance.

The gender non-conforming writer, speaker and artist ALOK Vaid-Menon has talked about the moment they pierced their nose, and the reaction of their grandmother. 'My grandmother, who lived with me at the time, said, "How could you do this to me?"', says ALOK. 'What she was feeling on the surface is that, in our culture which is so family-orientated and collectivist, I was betraying her, but prioritising myself.'

Now, ALOK sees it from a different perspective. 'When she said, "How could you do this to me?", what she was also saying is, "How could you show me that freedom is possible?"' says ALOK. 'In watching and witnessing you own your own body, I have to confront that way I have outsourced that ownership to other people, to culture, to identity.'

It comes back to self-esteem, or the lack thereof, that can run through our bloodline, thanks to years of subjugation. 'So much of the trauma we experience from our own people, comes from these histories of unprocessed trauma that made them feel like they were never enough,'[2] they add.

## ▷ Taking Responsibility

I don't want it to sound like I'm wandering my way through this book pointing the finger of blame and shirking responsibility. Part of past life parenting, in my experience, is taking full responsibility for the part you have played in all your lives, including this most recent one.

When I was writing this book, I hurt my hip from falling off my skateboard. It was the first longer-term injury that I've experienced. I have no doubt that, after researching this book, the timing was not a coincidence. So much of the frustration and fear I have felt around that injury (hello health anxiety!) has led me deeper into my research and my own healing journey.

I am lucky to have a group of very intuitive, female friends. Even a few months ago, I wouldn't have called on them for support, but it turns out I have made progress. On this day, I reached out to my friend Fleur Chambers, a meditation teacher and author of the books *10 Pathways* and *Wholehearted Confidence*. As I explained to Fleur, this injury was particularly triggering because my dad was paralysed from a tumour around his lower spine when I was a teenager.

'Is there a window here to connect with your dad?' asked Fleur. 'Energetically, there's some healing there to be done. Could you sit with the pain in your lower back and allow it to be a portal to understanding your dad's experience and offering him some compassion.'

At the time, my relationship with my dad was tricky. This was coming off the back of the pandemic when we'd been in lock-down in different countries. Like everyone in the world, it was a tense time, and had brought up a lot of old memories, especially around tough times in my family when I was a teenager. Even though my injury was caused by a skateboard fall, was it hanging around because I needed to heal something deeper? This was less about the physical pain which was actually very minimal (practically unnoticeable if I wasn't thinking about it). The symptom was the panic I felt around the injury and how this 'imperfection' in my body made me feel so incredibly vulnerable.

So, I decided to take Fleur's advice. That evening, and every evening for three weeks, I sat in meditation after my kids had gone to bed. I listened to a *Muladhara* root chakra meditation, which involves chanting the mantra '*Lam*' 108 times. (It's said, the *Lam* sound cleanses the root chakra of blockages.)

I also told my dad what I was doing and sent him a Spotify link to the chant so that he could choose to meditate at the same time as me, 7pm in Australia and 10am in England. As I meditated, I imagined energy swirling around my lower back until a portal opened around my spine—a portal that connected me to my father.

For the first few days, I just thought about myself. How sad I felt. How alone I felt. How judged I felt. But, on the fourth day something shifted. I received the message: 'You can make the men in your life feel unsafe'. I saw, not only my dad, but also my husband—the two major men in my life—and the impact that I had on their feelings of safety.

When I came out of that meditation, I sat down to journal what I had experienced. This is what I wrote in my notebook:

*'I'm always going on about not having a secure attachment style. But, right before Dad's illness I'd had my bad patch with my mum, and my eating disorder took a firm hold. How would that have made Dad feel? His sense of control; his safety; his root chakra?'*

When I was a teenager, right before my dad got sick, my eating disorder had hit its peak. My relationship with my mum was also going through a rocky patch. How would that have made my dad feel? What about his own feelings of familial stability? What would that have brought up from his childhood? How would it have triggered memories from his own father?

It's a long-running joke in my family that you never know what I'm going to do next. I can be spontaneous in a way that borders on erratic. I think it's partly a reaction to my first husband's death and the year that I spent being his fulltime carer. Without a doubt, it was too much responsibility for someone so young.

It's also just part of my personality. My husband always says that he half expects me to pack up and change my mind about our life at any moment. It's a long-running joke, but it's also not funny. How does that impact the stability of the people around me?

It might sound like I'm shaming myself, but this felt different. I admit, this realisation was a lot to process. Yes, I felt sad, but I didn't feel shame. Instead of self-criticism, I leaned into curiosity. I gained clarity around the relationship that I wanted to create with my own babies, my family, and my husband. I began to focus on what I wanted to create, not what I'd lost. Security and safety. Consistency and devotion. A trust that I'd always been there for my kids, even when they're pushing my buttons.

The experience was a reminder that we're all linked on a deeper level, especially the souls in our family (whether it's a blood family or chosen family). It reminds me of an incredible interview with the poet, Andrea Gibson, on the podcast, *We Can Do Hard Things* with author Glennon Doyle[3]. At the time, Andrea had just been told their ovarian cancer had returned and was categorised as terminal. In the interview, they spoke about their own spirituality and a special connection with their father, which manifested in a way they never expected.

'When I first started going through chemo, I lost every hair on my body except for my eyebrows,' says Andrea. 'I didn't talk about it—the fact I still had my eyebrows. My mother called me up one morning and said, 'You'll never believe what happened this morning? Your father woke up with his right eyebrow missing.' My dad has been missing his right eyebrow ever since I started chemo, and I kept my eyebrows.' Is it a cute and quirky coincidence or a clue to something bigger? For Andrea, it was a reason to believe in miracles and magic, even in difficult circumstances. As they put it: 'I guess it's the science of love.'

As I write this, my hip injury is healed. Just an echo is there, which only emerges when I feel emotionally vulnerable. As I wrote in my journal on that day, 'There is still healing to do on this timeline. I can feel it ... for Dad, for me and my babies.' Any kind of recovery doesn't have to feel like regret. A new revelation, even if it's a tough truth, doesn't have to feel like a failure. Looking into my pain and taking responsibility for my role is an important part of my healing, a part which only shows progress.

Glennon Doyle said: 'Any invitation to recover is a cosmic honour.' At the time, she was speaking about her eating disorder, but it's true of any recovery. 'I feel honoured by it when it happens,' explained Glennon on her podcast. 'To me, it's God, your universe, your people or whatever you call it, looking at you and all your coping mechanisms that you decided you needed to survive. And saying, "She's ready. She's ready now to live without this blockage. She wasn't ready before."'[4]

I spent 20 years not thinking about how my dad's cancer impacted him. Because it was too hard to see him as anything more than my dad—as a scared, broken being who didn't know if he'd survive this. A regular guy who felt the pain of his daughter's eating disorder; a little boy who felt the fragility of his family fracturing.

To move forward in my healing, I needed to go back. To strengthen my own stability, I needed to strengthen his stability. Interestingly, in the weeks after I did this meditation, my little boy's behaviour totally transformed. We went from having to manage his moods to watching him self-regulate, search out his own soothing tools and ask for help when he needed it.

It felt like I hadn't only rippled healing to my dad, but that I'd healed something in all of the men that I love. From the outside it did feel like my son had a new level of stability and safety. As I write this, I don't know how long it will last but, for this pocket of peace, I am grateful. The work was worth it.

## Chapter 11 ▷ Thinking Points

▷ We can all choose to 'surrogate' shadows for our ancestors—guilt, shame, fear, or any negative imprint, which they didn't have the resources to work through.

▷ If this feels true to you, how are you going? Do you feel like you've made progress? Is surrogating this shadow still serving you?

▷ When you're with your family, how do you sense negative emotions in your body? What clues are these feelings trying to tell you?

▷ Think back to your family history, way back through generations and generations. Sit with it. Feel all the feelings that never got felt, even if they aren't yours. But don't attach to them because that is not who you are.

# Chapter 12:
# Co-Parenting from Different Pasts

*How can you love every version of your partner, past and present, and still stay in love with yourself?*

Do you ever look at your partner—the person you created a family with—and think, 'Wow, we really see the world differently.' I think about it frequently in relation to my own partner, and it's not just because we were born in different countries and pronounce 'yoghurt' and 'garage' differently. All of us are a tapestry of our cultural and societal upbringing, family imprint, positive and negative experiences, and early influences. Then we take our tapestry and stitch it to another tapestry—our partner. No wonder it's not always a seamless alignment.

When I met my current partner I instantly knew that he was someone I needed to spend time with, whatever it took to make that happen. Now I understand more about soul recognition, it makes perfect sense to me. I recognised him as someone vital to my evolution, not to mention contentment (and we always had chemistry!). Despite this, we are very, very different people. I am a heart-led, trauma-rich pot of bubbling emotions, who grew up in London and then spent years not making a home anywhere. He is a logical and practical tree-trunk of stability who values loyalty over everything and loves nothing more than exploring the wilderness of his home country.

Of course, the differences in us make up the best of us. But, in the 'Debate Club' that is co-parenting, it can also turn the simplest decisions into a communication breakdown. How do we react to this child's tantrum? Do we get them Maccas drive-through again? Why don't we ever get a babysitter? What do we tell them about the tooth fairy? That's before you even get to the big stuff. Last week, I tried to explain the concept of 'white privilege' to my six-year-old. The week before, I attempted to explain to my husband why virginity is a social construct, whilst he listened with a 'here we go again' look on his face.

When it comes to the big-ticket items—discipline, sex, money, politics, life-after-death—how do your views compare to and contrast with your partners? If they clash, it's not surprising. In this lifetime alone we've all had such different journeys. Now, add in the possibility that you've had multiple lifetimes before this one. That's a lot of contrasting experiences that you're trying to integrate into one harmonious family unit.

Yet, we all know that the best teams are made up of diversity. Diverse teams are smarter, more innovative, and better at solving problems. Diverse teams are more creative. When people come from different backgrounds, have a variety of life experiences, and see the world in unique ways, these multiple perspectives create amazing aha-moments. It's true in the boardroom and in my experience, it's true in the bedroom. And it is in the bedroom that you started your family in the first place (or, in our case, in a tent on the edge of a rainforest ... but that's another story).

I would certainly not want to be married to myself, but it's also difficult to co-parent with my opposite. So, how can we parent peacefully, even when our pasts are so different? It comes back to the constant message in this book: it helps to see our people for the full spectrum of their experiences; to trust their instincts whilst still holding our own 'no' when we need to. I know, I know, it's not always that simple ...

▷ **The New Blended Families**

When we talk about blended families, we usually refer to a family unit where parents have children from previous relationships. In a way, however, we're all part of a blended family—a collection of souls, who've all fallen in love, fallen out of love, birthed babies and said goodbye to them. So, how does that impact our ability to live in love in this lifetime?

Side note: I purposefully used the phrase: live in love. For me, that is very different to 'falling' in love or even 'being' in love. In previous relationships I have acted in love without being in love. In my current relationship I have been in love without living in love or acting in love. You can only live in love when your walls are down. If your walls are up, you can only live beside love, not inside it.

If you look at your family unit like a basic maths equation, you might see two carers and two children (or a less cliched number if your family is more contemporary). But, if you see your family through a past life lens, it suddenly looks very different. Four souls with five lives each, for example. That's 25 lifetimes living under one roof. Does anyone else feel claustrophobic?

We often talk about the baggage that we bring from earlier relationships, meaning our sexual partners in this lifetime. But, what about all the lifetimes we've had before this one and how that plays a part in how we love, learn, fight, f*ck, and find our way as a partnership? According to past life and reincarnation specialist, Doctor Toni Reilly many of our relationships are impacted by the 'emotional bruises' we carry into this life, which can impact how we act, react and engage with each other.

Dr. Reilly began exploring past life healing after giving birth to three highly sensitive children. At the time, she was also going through a divorce and wanted to better support her family. After training with Doctor Brian Weiss, author of *Many Lives, Many Masters*, she overcame her own crippling fear of public speaking through past life therapy—and hasn't looked back since.

When Dr. Reilly works with clients of all ages, she focuses on their 'emotional bruises' and their causes. As she explains, 'The reason we reincarnate is to experience emotion—it's the human experience. We're born with certain emotional bruises, which are meant to happen.' Every person usually has one bruise that overrides the rest. When it's an emotional bruise, it defines the way that you behave; the way that you respond to criticism; the way that you form relationships. According to Dr. Reilly, the five emotional bruises are:

▷ abandonment
▷ rejection
▷ betrayal (trust issues)
▷ humiliation; and
▷ injustice.

Our bruises are usually formed in this life, she says, but often they'll be the same bruises that we've experienced in a past life. When that happens, it can feel even more raw and impactful. In one session, she regressed an adult male who recalled three past lives, which all had the theme of rejection in different ways.

*Rejection 1:* In the first life, he was a woman born in Venice in the 1600's; born to a wealthy family who wanted a son, not a daughter. In that life, her parents never got over the disappointment.

*Rejection 2:* In the second life, he lived in Mexico and was cast aside by an entire village for being a 'simpleton'.

*Rejection 3:* In the third life, he was a female performer living in London in the 1960's and was ostracised for being gay. In that life, she was rejected by her girlfriend, who chose to live a 'mainstream' life and went on to marry her ex-boyfriend.[1].

After their session, the client did some research and found an image from the 1960's of St Martin's Lane in London—an area close to the West End theatre district—which looked just like the image that he was shown in his regression. Of course, becoming aware is just the first step—you then have to do the work to put a 'pause' between a trigger and a reaction. When I met my current husband, I'd freak out every time he was 30 minutes late from work because I expected him to be involved in a fatal car crash at any moment. It was a trauma-response to losing my first husband. I discovered that it was my responsibility to bring myself back to reality. So, when I was triggered, I began to ask myself: What's more likely to be true? What's the most obvious (and boring!) explanation?

Another important reminder: past life hang-ups are not an excuse for toxic behaviour. Our emotional bruises can, however, explain the niggling, annoying fights that underpin a lot of co-parenting dynamics. Arguing about your kids' bedtimes in front of your in-laws. The division of labour. Why they packed a peanut butter sandwich in the school lunchbox. Why you're not having 'enough' sex. The fact they went on a work trip … and dared to enjoy it! Here's another way to look at these arguments and the emotional bruises that it could correlate with:

- ▷ Arguing about your kids' bedtimes in front of your in-laws → humiliation
- ▷ The division of labour → injustice
- ▷ Why they packed a peanut butter sandwich in the school lunchbox → betrayal (trust issues)
- ▷ Why you're not having 'enough' sex → rejection.
- ▷ The fact they went on a work trip and dared to enjoy it! → abandonment

For me, you don't have to know the exact set of events in their past that caused this bruise to be created in the first place (although, if you do, it can help it to become clearer). It's more about acknowledging that what you're arguing about probably isn't what you're arguing about ... because you can't solve a problem when you don't know the problem.

The world-renowned psychologist, Doctor Sue Johnson, the founder of Emotionally-Focussed Couples Therapy, talks about 'raw spots' (which sound very similar to Emotional Bruises). We all have raw spots. They are sensitivities that come from our temperament, our personal attachment histories, and from negative experiences in our relationship with our previous partners and current partner.

You can tell when one of your raw spots has been hurt because there is a sudden shift in the emotional tone of the conversation. She writes: 'You and your love were joking just a moment ago, but now one of you is upset or enraged, or, conversely, aloof, or chilly ... The hurt partner is sending out new signals, and the other tries to make sense of the change.'

It happens all the time in our house. I'm the first to admit that I'm a complex soul. Now I'm a lot more aware of my raw spots but, in the past, I could be triggered by the slightest wrong word slotted into a conversation. It might not sound like a lot of fun but exploring this idea doesn't have to feel heavy. When you're feeling connected (not when you've had an argument!), you could even chat about it with your partner. Which emotional bruise feels truest for them and you? Can you think of the strangest, even silliest, way it's shown up in your relationship, most-likely, in an argument? How are your bruises stopping you from getting close to each other?

The first place we can start is with a dose of compassion. If it's true that you've spent previous lifetimes with your partner, perhaps playing different roles in your family, then no wonder it feels messy sometimes. We're all entangled, but that's part of our grand evolution. It really comes back to one of the main messages of the book: how can you see the people you share a house, and a life, with for all that they are, and all that they've been?

## ▷ Valuing their Values

Sometimes, I use past life concepts to trick myself into being nicer to my partner. I'll give you a recent example. Every Anzac Day we take our family to the dawn service. If you're not familiar with the Australian tradition, Anzac Day is the annual day of commemoration in Australia and New Zealand for victims of war and for recognition of the role of their armed forces. It starts with a dawn service, which kicks off, as the name suggests, at dawn. Where we live it's very special—hundreds of people from our town gather at the local harbour under the flashing light of a lighthouse, with the crashing waves of the ocean in the background.

It's magical and memorable ... but there are downsides. It means that we must wake our kids up at 4.30am! It's also held every year on my son's birthday, which means we're usually hosting a party that afternoon. Let's just say, it's a lot, and it often ends in tears and tantrums.

Early in our relationship I realised that it was very important for my husband to attend every Anzac Day dawn service. Aside from the year I was giving birth, it's a non-negotiable. When we had tiny babies I would feel quite (very!) grumpy and quite (very!) resentful. Did it really matter if we missed a year when sleep was such a rarity? Then, one day, my husband mentioned that he had a recurring dream that he was on the front lines of battle. He could smell the stench of the trenches. He could see the artillery and the tanks so clearly. I don't even know if he can remember telling me about these dreams. But, from that moment on, I never begrudged going to dawn service again.

I choose to believe that my husband was a serviceman in a past life and that the dreams he has are the remnants of a memory. Am I right? Who knows? Call it a 'past life placebo effect' but it works for me. It's a fast-track to acceptance, understanding and patience. Even though this year was a disaster, and my kids started to argue as soon as we got to the lighthouse, we'll still set an alarm next year. I won't even complain ... well, not too much!

I've previously mentioned that my husband is incredibly loyal. He also highly values friendship (or 'mateship' as they say in Australia, to refer to male friendship). Coming from the transient, nomadic life I've led, this hasn't always been high on my priority list. This means that I can be quick to dismiss it. I can also quickly feel abandoned if I perceive that he's choosing his mates above me.

According to the relationship therapist Esther Perel couples polarise around all kinds of different values. It might sound like you're arguing about an everyday event ('why is it me who has to read all the school emails?') but it's actually the value underneath it we should focus on. She warns that modern romance doesn't pay much attention to 'values clarification' until there is a 'value crisis'.[2] In other words, we don't talk about our values as a couple until they clash, and it causes a problem.

So, how can we get ahead of it? Even if you don't believe in this past life thing (if that's the case, congrats on making it this far!), then it can help to just see the big picture.

▷ What is the value behind a reaction?

▷ What were the experiences that led to these values?

▷ Why does this value matter so much to your partner?

▷ And/or why does it matter so little to you?

▷ Check out a list of values in Appendix for inspiration.

If you're in a loving relationship most of us don't aim to frustrate our partner. My husband has always said to me, 'If there are two ways to take something and one of them is positive, you can assume that's where I'm coming from.' That can feel like you're giving a loved-one a lot of leeway, but it has brought greater harmony to my relationship.

Even when my husband does something I see as 'wrong', he is usually trying to do something 'right' in his eyes. And I know that, at the end of the day, we are aligned when it comes to 'our' moral compass. I put greater weight on values such as ambition, independence, and self-determination. He greatly values loyalty, leadership, and generosity. We both value adventure, freedom, love, learning and service. Sometimes we just take different routes to get there and this can be driven by our past experiences. Underneath it all, there's a lot of love.

In reality, sometimes, you don't see the big picture until a long time after an event or an argument. Remember how the medium, Laura Lynn-Jackson explained that there are some things in life we won't understand until the end of this life? In an ideal world, we don't have to end a relationship to put the pieces together.

A few months after I met my husband, in the first throws of our romance, he told me that he planned to go to South America for six months. He was clear: he was going with me or without me. At the time, I remember feeling a little offended. I couldn't take six months off work (my value: ambition). He hates to change plans once he's made them (his value: consistency). There was no wiggle room in the conversation. And, yes, I ended up going with him.

A few years later, during a past life regression, I learnt that my husband had been a medicine man in Peru. And that it was important for him to return to Peru so that he could move forward. It was in the mountains of Peru that he proposed to me after a ceremony in which we gifted our past back to *Pachamama*, mother earth, and asked for guidance in our future. He hadn't planned to propose that day, he always says, but something just came over him!

▷ **Rebirthing Within a Relationship**

When I was a teenager I remember counting down the weeks and days to the end of high school. I couldn't wait to move onto a new place; full of new people; a chance to recreate myself; to be whoever I wanted to be with people who didn't know who I was before. I carried this attitude forward into my adult life. I understand now it comes from a place of 'not enoughness'.

When I feel judged or criticised (by other people or myself), my instinct is to move on as fast as possible. I've done it with friends. I've done it with members of my own family. I'm working on it ...

For me, having kids has been the best stabilising influence in this area because I know I'll never leave them—it's out of the question. Yet when I feel vulnerable I can still veer into fantasies of a 'great reset'. My husband has said that if we ever split up, he knows I'll be fine. 'You'll just entirely recreate yourself,' he says. I do love a personal reinvention ... but I'd much rather do it with him.

I started this book with the statement: 'the point of life is to rebirth yourself over and over again'. The truth is, that can feel a lot harder when you're in a committed, long-term relationship; to evolve with a person who knows you inside out and who fell in love with an earlier version of you. But I do believe that it is possible.

After having kids, it might feel like your partner (or you) is a different person. But, as Esther Perel says, look beneath the surface. Do you have the same values in a different form? Do your values still align with each other's, even if they're slightly different? Do you still feel safe with each other? (This last one is a breadcrumb for a revelation in the next chapter).

I don't agree with people who say: I don't care about my partner's past. You should! Not from a place of criticism or judgement, but from a place of curiosity, compassion, and amazement. As epigenetics has found, our past trauma doesn't change our DNA per se, but it does change how our genes are 'expressed'; whether and how they release the information they're carrying. I am not the sum of my past experiences but my past does impact how I express myself.

On a day when I'm lit up, when you see the sparkle in my eye, that's because of the stuff I've survived. On the day when I'm in shadow, that's because of the stuff I'm still surviving. And the future is for 'us' both to navigate together.

I can't bounce back to the person that I was before I was a baby, any more than I can 'bounce back' to the version of me who died drinking contaminated water. That doesn't mean we can't miss things about ourselves or our partners. The American philosopher, Sam Harris says, 'within spirituality you still need to teach people how to grieve.'[3] That's true of every loss we face, whether it's the death of a loved-one's physical body or the end of a season of a relationship.

I remember one therapy session talking about my fear of my daughter growing up, because we're so conditioned as mothers to dread it happening. My therapist said, 'your child growing up is never just a loss—something is always gained.' Imagine if we could have the same attitude to our partners, and to ourselves? The point of life is to rebirth yourself over and over. So, how can we learn to do it together?

When I met my current husband, I felt like a high-flying journalist always chasing an exciting or glamorous story. Every week, I had a different headline in a newspaper or a magazine. I'd send him clips from my latest TV appearances. It was a season of my career, which was easy to outwardly validate and felt great for my ego. Today, I am in a softer era of life—making decisions based on how it feels for our family and our collective nervous system. Because of this, I can feel less-than. It's easy to devalue what you bring to your family when it's less shiny than your previous life purpose. But, when I don't shut myself down, I can see this latest version of me is invaluable to us.

Last week, after my husband had had a few difficult weeks at work, I invited him on a 'date'. No movie. No sex. An energy clearing ritual where I created a cocoon in our bedroom and asked him to lay on our bed so I could shift his energy. For the next 20 minutes, I followed my intuition, using all the skills that I've learnt during this 'hippier' season of my life. The ability to read energy. The ability to read feelings in others. The ability that we all have, to heal with our hands. The innate knowledge of how to clear emotional blockages in another person. (Many of the innate skills that we start to doubt and devalue during our childhoods.)

Not only did it help my husband and allow us to connect on a sensual level, but the next day I noticed an unexpected consequence. When my little boy got in bed with me the next morning, instead of kicking and writhing as he usually does, his body was perfectly calm. He was chatty, but peaceful. The energy around his body felt completely different.

Previously, when I interviewed Peter Smith, I had asked his advice on how to navigate my relationship with my son when it feels like we're so, deeply connected (too connected, it can feel, at times). At the time, Peter offered this guidance, 'That's something for the two of you—and the three of you—to learn as part of your soul contract in this life, most likely.' He was talking about me, my son and my husband, and how navigating our complex relationship was part of our soul contract.

It was an important reminder. I have the capacity for all the loves in my life. When I tap into my gifts, I can be everything they need me to be. During that healing ritual, I had sent healing throughout the love triangle that is us. And I had soothed my son without even being near him, whilst he was asleep in another bedroom. We are all entangled, and that's part of the grand lesson in love.

## Chapter 12 ▷ Thinking Points

▷ How can you appreciate, rather than begrudge, the diversity of heart and minds in your family? How can you start to value your differences, and fall back in love with them?

▷ Read over the five emotional bruises (abandonment, rejection, trust issues, humiliation, and injustice) and consider which ones are at the core of most of your arguments.

▷ Chat to your partner about your values and how they may differ. I've included a list of Core Values in the Appendix. Go through them alone or together, and see which ones jump out for you.

▷ How many lives have you had inside this one relationship?

▷ How can you and your partner support each other to rebirth constantly, and still choose each other?

# Chapter 13:
# Parenting without Shame

*In a culture of rules, a mother without shame is a revolution.*

▷ For me, one of the most toxic emotions that a child or a parent can feel is shame. Yet it seems to be so ingrained in our culture's DNA that it can become the default emotion we experience. By this point in the book, I hope that you've taken steps to ease any misplaced shame you have around your child and their behaviour; to appreciate and accept all that they are; to avoid comparing and critiquing; to trust their own instinct to guide them, even if it goes against what society expects of them. But, what about yourself?

Almost two thirds of mums have felt shamed over their parenting choices. A survey found that 61 per cent of mothers reported receiving criticism about their parenting decisions—largely from their co-parent, their in-laws, or their own parents. Surprisingly, mothers reported receiving less criticism from their friends, other mothers they come across in public, and even social-media commenters, than their own families.[1]

It's not only our present-day choices we feel ashamed about. It seems that 'mum guilt' extends to our actions in an earlier part of our timeline. After having kids, we can get nostalgic about our past—and not always in a good way. Our past relationships; our past sex lives; the decisions we made which could be seen as 'risky' or, if you have daughters, un-feminist!

We wonder what we'll tell our kids when they get older about our exes, our choices, or how we ended up losing our clothes and our passport one fateful night in Ibiza. I'm writing this as a thrice married woman (widowed, divorced and happily married to my babies' daddy). In many ways I have spent a lifetime defending my past choices, partly because I've spent my career writing about them publicly. As my oldest daughter neared her seventh year, realising that this was a pivotal time for the creation of her self-identity, I knew that it was time to really address my own 'Shame Centre'.

Imagine your Shame Centre as a call centre. For me this is easy—I used to work in a call centre selling double-glazed windows when I was a teenager. Except that this Shame Centre is inside your body, maybe your chest or near your belly. It's full of people on telephones trying to convince people to buy into what they're selling. They sound convincing, but they're just reading a script. A script probably written by a middle-aged, white man. For a long time, you've believed the script, even if it hasn't felt right in your heart. Because the salespeople are convincing. And they're confident. And you keep hearing the same sales pitch over and over, until you feel forced to buy into it. This is what my personal Shame Centre tries to sell me, even now that I'm a doting mother in my late thirties. Tell me if it sounds familiar!

▷ *You were a terrible teenager.*
▷ *You tore your family apart.*
▷ *You make it difficult to love you.*
▷ *You were a slut.*
▷ *You made terrible life choices.*
▷ *You only have value now, because you're in a committed relationship (e.g. you're not a slut anymore).*

▷ *You're selfish.*
▷ *You better hope your children don't end up like you.*

Like all of us, my Shame Centre script comes from multiple sources. Some of the criticism is imagined and has only ever existed in my mind. Some has actually been said to me over the years, either by people I loved, by people I barely knew, or by complete strangers.

Thanks to therapy, I'm not such an easy sell anymore. I know how to challenge these thoughts and look for alternative evidence, which shows that I am loved, cherished and valued. But until this point, it has felt like a lot of hard work to silence the chatter of my Shame Centre, especially when I'm overwhelmed or sleep deprived.

I also never thought to look back further. Is it possible I've carried forward shame from earlier in my timeline? For me, this became a life-changing turning point in writing this book. Yes, we're getting weirder—but it's going to be worth it!

## ▷ **WTF is Repatterning?**

After a decade of working in the spiritual, new-age space, I thought I'd heard everything about past lives and soul healing. But it wasn't until I started researching this book that I heard about 'Nun Karma'. Nun Karma is a 'repatterning process' which aims to help people, especially women, to release lifetimes of 'limiting solemn vows' made as nuns, monks and renunciates. The idea is that many of us would have taken 'vows' in our previous lives as part of our vocations, jobs, or identities.

If you were a nun, for example, you might have taken a vow of celibacy, silence, or poverty. Some of these patterns serve us and others hold us back. Imagine that you're going about your life now—in a post-pill society where sexuality is fluid. Is there an inner conflict between your old vows and this way of living?

This is where 'Resonance Repatterning' comes in—a way to create a bridge between releasing unwanted vows (especially the vow of poverty) and create meaningful lives and professions in the 21st Century. The idea is that you 'renounce' your old vows and then create new ones—vows that better serve you. Side note: If the idea of Nun Karma is intriguing to you, I followed a formula created by certified practitioners of the Repatterning System[2]. This formula is open-source, so I am free to share it with their permission. You can download the full guide, Nun Karma, on my website, *amymolloy. com.au/pastlifeparenting*.

As I went through the process, I discovered that I didn't identify with the life of a nun. I did, however, identify with two other roles which are associated with making and breaking vows—a martyr and a prostitute. This is where I should point out: I am aware the word 'prostitute' is a derogatory phrase. I initially considered changing it to 'sex worker', but I wanted to stay true to the Nun Karma original wording. If we are talking about my past life and the impact of that role, it felt truer to use the slur and acknowledge its historical baggage.

You might also be asking: what does sex work have to do with vows? According to the process, it is a 'flip side of nun and monk karma'. For example, if you practised a life as a prostitute, it could still impact your experience of celibacy, obedience, and service. One of the reasons the word 'prostitute' is not politically correct today because it was originally used as a verb. To 'prostitute' wasn't a thing one did, it was something done to you. When I went through the process to identify the vows I had taken, they included:

▷ **Silence**—I cannot raise my voice or speak out loud on my own behalf.

▷ **Obedience**—I obey the Mother – Bishop – Abbot – Head Priest without question.

▷ **Martyrdom**—I believe in self-sacrifice.
▷ **Penance**—to purify my body from sin, I fast or self-flagellate. I enjoy doing penance.

That hit a nerve! It certainly lined up with some of my coping mechanisms in this life—undereating, overworking, silencing my needs and when I did speak my truth, feeling like I was deserving of the backlash. As I've said, the Nun Karma process is very lengthy. For me, it ended with creating 'new vows' to replace my old ones. As my guide said, 'In the vacuum created by the release of old vows, there is ample room for inserting new vows in terms of beliefs, behaviours, goals and soul purpose.'

To 'strengthen your vows', it's recommended you read them out loud once a day, whilst tapping on the temples or the sides of your face. The tapping is a version of the Emotional Freedom Technique (EFT), which is meant to strengthen neural pathways. I've included my vows at the end of this chapter. You can read through them and see if they speak to you. If they do, feel free to adopt them as your own and see if it creates any shifts in your mindset.

At the time of writing this chapter, I'm six weeks into my daily practice and despite my earlier scepticism, I'm a convert. Even my husband has noticed a difference. You don't have to believe in past lives to see the benefits of breaking vows that you've made with yourself. All our values and belief systems shift and change as we get older, especially when we become parents. Do they still serve you? Or is it time you renounced them? Call it past lives or call it the placebo effect but I can see the impact of breaking my vows every day.

*Silence*. As I work on a TV show about my first book, *Wife Interrupted,* I'm letting myself feel the grief of the backlash that I faced for writing about my sex life. I've cried more tears for that period than I've ever cried. I'm finally standing up for that 23-year-old version of me who was hung, drawn and quartered for dealing with grief through sexuality.

*Obedience.* When I'm making decisions for my family, my default isn't to think about the opinion of my own mother, or any other females in my life, and whether they will approve of it. On reflection, I've spent my whole adult life searching for a series of 'mother figures'. How can I love them without fearing their opinion?

*Martyrdom.* When my daughter's school calls to tell me that she's in the sick bay, I still put down the phone and say 'F*CK', but then I choose to make the best of it. Instead of suffering for the sake of suffering, I make a cosy nest on the couch, and we watch TV together. Or I ask my husband to be the sick kid parent.

As for *penance* ... I am allowing myself to realise that life is to be enjoyed, and that I am part of an amazing family that I'm allowed to be proud of. I even changed my computer password to the final sentence of my new vows. It's a powerful daily reminder: *'It's great to be me'.*

## ▷ Shame + The Seven Year Cycle

As we've discussed in earlier chapters, the area of epigenetics is starting to show the impact of past trauma, including our ancestor's trauma, on our own DNA. And how the trauma experienced by our ancestors can turn into disease or disorder in our bodies.

A year before writing this book, I had an experience which reminded me of the link between our emotions and our physical body. Out of the blue, I heard that one of my ex-partners was sick—he'd recently been diagnosed with cancer. My dad, who is in remission from cancer, told me the news. At the time I was in therapy to deal with residual trauma from my first husband dying from cancer. Let's just say I felt like I couldn't escape the C-word.

The morning after I heard the news I woke up to a searing pain in my stomach and my chest. The closest medical diagnosis was gastritis—inflammation of the lining of the stomach, but I felt like I was dying. For over a week I couldn't ease the pain. My parents were visiting from London, and I remember sitting on the edge of their bed, sobbing. What was happening to me? I felt out of control. My body felt like it was betraying me.

As luck would have it, I had a Zoom call booked with my spiritual healer in London, so I asked her: 'Why is this happening to me? How can I stop it?' This is what I wrote down during that session:

*'The shock of the news has reverberated through your body.'*

*'That part of your body is all about what you can control in life and what you can't 'digest'.'*

*'The shock is because it took you back to your first husband—there's another man in my life with this disease—three men I've been intimate with on a loving vibration.'*

*'We must try and clear this panic reaction you get to illness or cancer.'*

'We can carry in our cellular body every shock we've ever had—it doesn't take much to open it again.'

It felt like I was reflecting my ex-partner's disease in my own body, or at least translating the panic I felt at the news into a physical sensation. I realised that I had to stop being a passive victim and take back my power by understanding my role in our shared situation. Here are more notes I made during that session:

*People go into victim mode.*

*Panic settles into an organ. You don't want that to happen.*

*You can't take on the karma of other people's journey and apply it to yourself.*

*You are here to observe it, to learn from it, not to live it.*

*You can heal yourself by changing your mindset.*

*I am strong.*

*I am healthy.*

*This is someone else's story.*

Soon after that session, all my symptoms vanished. As my healer explained, it was an important lesson: we store our old traumas in our bodies, and it doesn't take much to reignite them. But we can break the cycle and say: *'I am not having this. I choose peace in my body.'*

Interestingly, my healer also explained that trauma can take seven years to work through your body (based on the belief that our cells regenerate every seven years). If you're experiencing illness, disease, or any unexplained symptoms, pause and think: what happened in my life seven years ago?

Seven years before I experienced these symptoms, I divorced my second husband. I didn't cry over that divorce because I didn't think I deserved to. Instead, I replaced the softness of sadness with the stickiness of shame. Shame, imagining my parents telling their friends that I had 'another' failed relationship. Shame that I'd have to explain my choices to my future partner and our future children.

Interestingly, when I left my second husband I wasn't focused on his forgiveness—I didn't know if that would ever be possible. But I already felt like I had one foot in the future: begging my future partner to love me despite my past ... not because of it.

Now, I understand the real impact of those emotions. When I left my second husband I sent waves of shame and guilt forward to my future—the future I'm living now with my husband and children. Today, when I feel waves of guilt and shame, it isn't my current husband making me feel that way. It's a younger version of me; standing with a suitcase on the street; feeling shame for bringing shame on her family. The good news is that it's never too late to send that shame back and stand up for yourself. You can even do it as you're sleeping (which is great news for exhausted parents!). Intrigued? Read on ...

## ▷ The Power of Lucid Dreaming

In my experience, time travel is real ... we do it constantly, all of us. Every time we think back on a past event, or we dwell on a time we were 'wronged', or we bitch about something that has happened to us, we transport ourselves back to that moment.

Do you know science has shown that our body can't tell the difference between a current threat and a memory? We react in the same way, releasing stress hormones like adrenaline and cortisol. Try it right now if you're a glutton for punishment. Imagine a stressful event in your past (but nothing too traumatic) and see the reaction it has on your body.

It's why the impact of Post-Traumatic Stress Disorder (PTSD) feels so real. And its why recovery can be so powerful—although it's not always easy. As someone who is in recovery from PTSD relating to my late-husband's death, I can tell you: our present healing *can* change our past experiences. With work, it can help you to forgive, to release, to rewire and reframe some of the things that have happened to you.

As I work on the TV show about my earlier life, and in doing so, confront some tough memories, I've been exploring the power of 'lucid dreaming'. Lucid dreaming is when you know you're dreaming, even when you're asleep. Instead of being totally immersed in a dream as if it is real, there is a moment when you think: this is only a dream. From there, you can become an observer and a curator— moving through your dream like a character in a computer game.

New research is examining the impact of lucid dreaming for people with PTSD. About 80 per cent of PTSD patients suffer from nightmares—repeated intense nightmares that most often centre on threats to physical safety and security.

Multiple studies have found that Lucid Dreaming Therapy (LDT) allows people to alter the story line of a nightmare during the dream phase.[3] For example, if you have nightmares about getting washed away in a tsunami, when you realise you are dreaming, you can alter the storyline—perhaps, you are rescued by a helicopter or you grow a mermaid>s tail and swim to safety.

Through lucid dreaming, some people choose to confront or forgive an attacker. It can also be a way to face a fear. If you frequently dream of getting sick, or one of your kids being hurt, how can you practise the optimum way to react in this situation?

How do you learn to lucid dream? It's a process that's too long to include in this chapter. I recommend the work of Charlie Morley, who wrote the book, *Lucid Dreaming: A Beginners Guide to Becoming Conscious in Your Dreams*. He coaches people to be able to 'wake up' in a dream and then to 'reframe' your dream's perspective. For instance, if you have a reoccurring dream of missing a school exam, can you soothe yourself in your dream? It's just one exam; you can retake it!

Can we teach our kids to lucid dream? Well, that all depends on their age. In fact, you might not need to teach them. Research has found that younger children have higher rates of lucid dreaming naturally (rates of lucid dreaming drop off around the age of 16).[4] One study found that lucid dreaming was reported by 58 per cent of six-year-olds, which surprised researchers.[5]

According to lucid dreaming mentor Stefan Zugor children don't need to be coached as much as adults. He recommends three steps for young people[6]:

▷ meditate every morning
▷ write your dreams down; and
▷ try to set the intention to lucid dream.

The third step is actually very simple. Before you go to bed, pause, and think: 'I'm going to lucid dream tonight.' Lucid dreaming also has the potential to help children who experience nightmares. In a dreamscape, they can 'dress rehearse' events in their life that scare them and experiment with different ways to react to them.

As I began to explore lucid dreaming, I had an interesting experience. Since becoming a mother, I've had a recurring nightmare. I'm surrounded by members of my family who are yelling at me, criticising me and condemning me, especially for things I did when I was younger. For many, many dreams, I just took it like a punching bag—and then I decided to change the narrative.

Before bed, I began to set an intention: 'If people I love are screaming at me in my dreams, I will know it's just a dream, and I will change the story.' From that moment on, whenever that dream came up, I knew it was a dream and I started to stand up for myself. Instead of taking the criticism, I began to talk back:

*'I won't let you talk to me like that.*
*That is not who I am.*
*I was not a bad child.*
*I've created a good life.*
*I'm a good mother.'*

Instead of waking up feeling broken, I began to wake up feeling bold, uplifted and defiant. As a side note, in a recent past life healing, I revisited a past life memory where my child was taken away from me for crimes I didn't commit. I say myself in a courthouse crying. Is this another reason, I feel like I constantly have to prove myself?

I am not someone who lives conflict in my waking life, but in my dreamscape I can do it. And that's been incredibly empowering. I'm still not great at standing up for myself in real life, but I know there's a part of my subconscious that will protect me—and that's good enough for now.

## Chapter 13 ▷ Thinking Points

▷ What scripts does your Shame Centre try to convince you are true about your life before you were a parent? Do you buy into it?

▷ Do you identify with any of these roles: nun, monk, martyr, priest, sex worker, witch/seductress, slave, servant, victim, abuser, or saviour?

▷ Is it possible that past life vows are stopping you from freely making money, forming relationships, or expressing yourself verbally, sexually, or creatively?

▷ What do your dreams have to say about how you feel about your past—and how can you start to stand up for your dream self?

### ▷ My New Vows

*If these vows call to you, try speaking to them out-loud once a day. To strengthen the vows, tap the side of your cheeks just under your eyes whilst you're saying them.*

I accept all the abundance that is mine in this lifetime. I am amply rewarded for everything I create. I accept with humility all the money that comes to me in this life.

As my self-esteem increases, I project my desirability as a mate, as a business partner, as an effective source of support, learning and healing for others.

I am free to speak out for myself in any situation. I speak, write, and freely make my needs, thoughts and desires known to others. What I say is respected and accepted.

I follow my heart's desires and soul's creative expressions.

I dress in my own colourful, unique style.

I enjoy radiating my natural sex appeal, smarts, and personality.

I can find perfect love because I discovered it first in myself.

It's great to be me.

And so it is ...

(Adapted from *Nun Karma*. A Free Open-Source Re-Patterning Formula created by Carol Cannon, Gail Glanville, Kathie Joblin, Nancy Martin, Carolyn Winter, Helene Zahn-Chilberg)

## Chapter 14:
# The Relief of a Timeless Life

*Before this life, during this life and after this life, I will always love you.*

▷ If I was to ask most parents about their greatest fear, it would be the loss of a child or the heartbreaking thought of saying goodbye forever. It can wake us in the night. It becomes a plotline in our dreams. It pops into our heads at the most inconvenient moment. I was sitting in our spa with my husband and another dad the other night, when the dad admitted that, sometimes, when he's driving, he gets a wave of fear around death that hits him out of nowhere and makes him almost inconsolable.

One of the gifts that researching this book has given me is that I have zero fears around death right now. I still have fear around the decline of my body in the lead-up to the end of this life but writing this book has erased any worries that I have around what's next for us, and replaced it with a feeling closer to excitement.

I do, however, share the eternal fear of parents: will we be given 'enough' time with our children? Enough time to memorise their faces; to see all their firsts; to guide their growth into adults; to survive the battle of the early years of parenting and move into a stage that feels softer, sweeter and easier to enjoy together.

I have a number of mum friends at the moment who are going through chemotherapy and I know their greatest heartbreak is the sense that time is running out for them. They feel heartbroken because they're spending so much time in treatment. Then there's the fear that the treatment won't work, and their life will end sooner than they ever imagined. Even thinking about this scenario makes our hearts ache as caregivers. This is why, in this chapter, I want to—and need to—gather some important lessons woven through this book into a final, revolutionary call-to-action.

Parents, mothers, fathers, carers ... we must crawl out of the shadow of time-scarcity that we live under and free ourselves from the shackles of a man-made creation. We must realise, and remember, that time is a social construct. Time isn't linear. Time isn't our prisoner. Time isn't inescapable. Time is a practical tool, which is helpful to catch the school bus and track nap times, but it should not be the measure of our success or our safety. We cannot allow it to become the monster in our nightmares or the warden that watches over us.

I know what you're thinking: how, how, how? In this chapter, I'm going to give you a new way to approach time, and how it fits into the pillars of Past Life Parenting. More importantly, I'll explain why I personally find a lot of relief and peace, by parenting from a 'timeless' place where there's always another shot, healing is never-ending and love truly is eternal. In releasing ourselves from time, we gain more time and make time eternal—and we never have to experience a 'last' day with our children.

## ▷ If Time is an Illusion, Why Does it Feel So Real?

If you believe in the Buddhist concept that we create our own suffering, then time really is the ultimate weapon, especially when you're a parent. How are you using 'time' against yourself right now?

In an average week (or day), this is how I use my understanding of time to self-flagellate with thoughts such as:

▷ You're wasting time — (when I dare to rest).

▷ It's too much time away — (when I drop my kids at childcare).

▷ You'll never get this done — (when I'm staring at a deadline).

▷ It's been three weeks — (when I'm feeling bad about my sex life).

▷ You'll never get this time back — (when I don't enjoy spending my day-off with my kids).

▷ How will I ever survive? — (when I worry about one of my children dying or the thought of saying goodbye to them forever).

When you dig down into most of our everyday worries and nightmares, how many of them are linked to our concept of time, and to the fierce belief that it's a one-way highway? 'There isn't enough of it. It's passing too fast. This is all going to be over before we're actually ready.' And, so, we suffer. We suffer because, to us, time is a limited resource, and we are locked into a scarcity mindset.

The problem is that time really isn't real. And it's actually a topic where spiritualists and scientists seem to agree. If one person thinks that a day has gone slowly, and another person thinks that a day has flown by, which one is correct? Neither, when you realise that all time is subjective. If you talk to a scientist about this, they'll point to Einstein's Special Theory of Relativity, which agrees— the fabric of time and space is relative. For a full explanation, I recommend reading Doctor Carl Rovelli's book, *The Order of Time*. In the first draft of this book, I attempted to give a breakdown of Quantum Physics, but it became a little ... wordy!

Of course, we can't ignore the fact that days pass into nights, but how can we feel less pressure around the passing of the seasons?

Even if you believe in rebirth, there's no denying that the movie that we call Life will reach its final credits eventually. Nevertheless, can we find a way to feel motivated and passionate about life, whilst removing the pressure of a ticking clock or a looming deadline?

The first way is to stop tracking time so closely. This can be hard for parents because our kid's lives are attached to a breakdown of milestones. They're 23-months-old. It's their first day of school. They lose their first tooth. It's their first night in a big-kid bed. It's their final year of school and their first date. Time is a constant in all our conversations. It happens from the moment we give birth when we compare our 'bounce-back' to the recovery of other mothers. One thing I do is to circuit-break the conversation. When someone gestures to my kids and says, 'It goes so fast', I don't just agree; I really stop and think. Does it feel fast to me?

I think of all the seasons of parenthood I've experienced since my babies were born, and all we've done as a family—big moments, small moments and everything in between. Usually, I reply something like, 'I actually don't think it's gone fast. It feels like I've lived lifetimes since they were born—it's wonderful.' We can't change a mindset until we break the loop of repetitive, automated, nay-saying conversations.

And we need to, because time is used as another reason to shame and detain mothers, in particular—but we deserve to be free of it.

One of my least-favourite memes, which frequently circulates on social media, is the threat (yes, I see it as a threat) aimed at mothers: 'You only get 18 summers with your kids, so don't waste any'. It cuts to your core when you're a stressed-out parent who wants to enjoy every moment with their children, but doesn't ... because that seems truly impossible. Time is a useful measure and a powerful teacher. It can help us to track our progress, mark our milestones and inspire us to create precious memories. But it can also trap us in misery and sadness, and make us miss the people that we love, even when we're still with them.

When it comes to unclenching our fist around the passing of time, our children can be our greatest teachers. Spending time with us is more valuable to them than any shop-bought product. But the actual number of minutes we spend with them matters less than our whole-hearted attention and presence (this will be especially true if they have any emotional bruises from a past life linked to abandonment).

When I pick up my three year old daughter from day-care, the six hours we've spent apart vanishes for her, in a moment. All she knows is, I'm back and she wants to relish that moment. Our kids look forward to the passing of time with excitement ('I can't wait until I'm 10 years old and I can have a Nintendo'). They wave goodbye to years with joy, wonder and exhilaration ... purely because nobody has told them to fear it. Imagine if we could all forget our conditioned fear of time, and hold it with less terror and, at least, a sense of neutrality?

I love what the spiritual teacher Sadhguru says about attachment. In Buddhism, and some other religions, we're encouraged not to be attached to anything (people, places, periods of our lives). This is impossible, says Sadhguru. We are attached because we care. The problem only comes when we are attached to things unequally. If we were equally attached to all people, places and periods of our lives, we wouldn't mourn so deeply if one is over or vanishes. So, be attached to the past, the present and the future—but be attached to all of them equally. When the past is over, we can welcome the present. When the future is over, we get to return to the start again.

## ▷ Firsts, Lasts & Freedom

When tech expert, Mo Gawdat was working as the Chief Business Officer at Google X, he lost his son, Ali, during a routine surgery. Now, as the author of multiple best-selling books on happiness, he says that he doesn't know what death is, but he believes that it's not a linear process. In a YouTube video, Mo shares his thoughts on life and loss:

*'If you truly understand the theory of relativity and space-time continuum, and truly understand that time doesn't exist in the way we think it does ... you have to start questioning: who died first? Me or Ali? Who lived first? Me or Ali? First or last is a property of the physical.'*[1]

Although Mo says that he avoids thinking too spiritually, what he believes does sound very comforting—that, without an observer, there is no time, space, or matter. Mo gives an everyday example: if you're standing inside a building, you can't see the building. You have to be standing outside the building to see it. 'The reason why we perceive time is because the real us resides outside space-time,' he says. 'This [body] is an avatar—this really is. This is the physical vehicle you use to navigate the physical world. You are sitting somewhere else with the control, otherwise you couldn't perceive it.'

So, what to think? We're here and somewhere else at the same time? Yes, according to almost every clairvoyant and past life regressionist that claims to have peaked behind the metaphysical curtain.

The medium, Laura Lynne Jackson says that there is 'a fluidity between the past, the future and the present'. According to Laura, her spirit guides explain it like this:

*'Do you know what a maypole is, like you'd see at a village fair? Your soul energy is the pole in the centre. It divides out into all the different coloured strings, but it all ties back together.'*

Confused? That's understandable! Laura says that the spirit guides joke that it's like teaching your dog algebra. Her overarching message? 'It's all happening at the same time,' says Laura. 'The lives you're having are all intertwined. Time is not linear.'[2]

Past life messenger, Michael Armstrong also agrees. It all links back to the vision that he saw in his spiritual epiphany—a ball of light with water droplets of light bouncing off it. 'There's only a fragment of our soul which is animating our human body at this time,' says Michael. 'The rest [of our soul] is in the spiritual realm, a timeless zone. That soul is capable of controlling two bodies.' He says the most important thing to realise is that our soul is much bigger than our body.

Why is this so incredibly important for parents, and how can it bring us a lifetime of comfort? In a timeless life, endings are not enduring. There isn't a question of who was born or dies first. Life is a series of beginnings and endings, which have already happened, are happening now, and will continue to happen in the future, simultaneously. Compared to the rigidity of linear time, which we're told is inescapable, this version feels spacious, liberating and exhilarating. I can simultaneously be with my children in this lifetime, whilst part of my soul is dancing with theirs in the aether. Also, if time isn't linear, the best parts of our life are never over because it's all happening simultaneously.

Right now, my children are aged three, five and six in this life. But, in another dimension of time, I'm about to give birth for the first time; to feel the power of pushing a baby out of my body and placing her cheek on mine. In another dimension of time,

I'm watching my little boy get married; I'm nursing my daughter through her first heartbreak; I'm saying goodbye to my children on my deathbed. It's all happening. It's all natural. It's all perfectly fine, and exactly as it's meant to be.

## ▷ The Best Bedtime Story has No Ending

We can all embrace this limitless version of time if we allow ourselves to turn away from the ticking clock and to trust it. Personally, after I sat with this mystical concept, and allowed myself to hold it lightly, it enabled me to breathe. Instead of dreading the passing of time and viewing each birthday as a threat to my happiness, I could smile at it.

All of this makes me a kinder, gentler mother because I'm less fearful and, therefore, less rigid. I can see my children and be present for all of their questions. At least three nights a week, as I tuck my six-year-old into bed, she asks me a question about what happens when you become a 'star in the sky'. Currently, she alternates between wanting to reincarnate as a baby human or a baby elephant. She also wants to be in the stars with me, her mummy. Sob! If the people I spoke to for this book are correct, she can get all her wishes—and I don't have to go to bed dreading our time together ending.

At the very least, let this (somewhat confusing!) concept be your cheerleader the next time someone tells you to seize every day with your children. I might only have 18 summers with my children in this ribbon of my maypole, but there are many more ribbons for us to twirl together through our lifetimes.

## Chapter 14 ▷ Thinking Points

▷ Where does your understanding of time come from, and how does a rigid idea of the concept of time make you suffer?

▷ How would parenting feel different (and maybe less pressured?), if you truly believed that time is not linear or concrete?

▷ If your soul is much bigger than your body, does that mean your capacity to love is infinite?

▷ If there's truly no first or last; no beginning or endings, how can you feel less fearful as a parent—and embrace every season of yours and your kid's lives?

▷ Can you give yourself permission right now to never fear the passing of time again? I dare you to try it!

## Chapter 15:
# Living for the Future

*There comes a time to tell your trauma: you are no longer a core part of my identity.*

▷   I find it interesting that, in all my research into past lives, very few people talk about their happy past life memories. In over 60 interviews on past life memories and countless hours of research, I uncovered a deluge of information on past life trauma; people who'd experienced loss, pain, abandonment, rejection, and all manner of hurtful experiences. But, what about our happy past life imprints?

It stands to reason that, if we're carrying forward hurtful memories, there has to be an echo of our happier, joyful moments. Surely! Is our Negative Bias—our tendency to cling to negative memories—so strong that we only have a soul imprint of our past suffering and not our contentment? And if that is the case, are we at risk of creating a Trauma Bond with a past life identity, and encouraging our children to feel like a victim?

In recent years, this is a topic that has become a bit of a passion project for me. Even before I began researching past life theory, I became interested in the role of our past experiences on our present-day happiness (and how we attach to our suffering). In my work as a journalist and editor, I have helped thousands of people to publicly share their toughest experiences, because I believe that sharing our struggles helps us to heal from them. But, there is a catch! We are at risk of becoming over-identified with one story, especially if that story is linked to adversity (because we live in a culture which glorifies struggle).

As I've said before, I am a fan of therapy and I do believe that, to move forward, it is important to look backwards ... to a point. We can, however, become a victim to the condition of Naval Gazing—self-indulgent or excessive contemplation of oneself. And, as my husband often says, 'Can we all stop taking life so seriously?' So, how can we access the wisdom of past life knowledge without getting lost in the people we used to be?

## ▷ Is it Bad to Look Back?

You might imagine that, as we come to the end of a 60,000-word book on past life parenting, my final advice would be to go and book a past life regression, pronto! Dive into your past; get hypnotised; spend the next three weeks staring in the rear-view mirror at your lifetimes. But, in my experience, like all aspects of therapy and self-development, we must find a balance between peering into the past for solutions ... and getting stuck in it.

When the spiritual author, Deepak Chopra, was asked about the benefits of past life-regression, he said this:

*'The reason we don't usually remember previous lives is because it is not helpful for our present growth. Too much memory only clutters and burdens the mind and draws attention away from the present moment where our consciousness needs to be.'*

According to Deepak, our everyday experiences of the present are made possible and coherent only because we filter out most of the data that comes into our senses. 'Without limiting our experience and our memories into what is useful and appropriate, we would be incapacitated with a deluge of information,' he says. 'It's not wrong to have an interest in life after death, but you need to ask yourself 'how is that interest helping you live your life more fully right now?''

I also think it's important to search out the good stuff. If, indeed, you do want to explore past life memories, then be aware of your inbuilt negative bias. If you're meditating on a past life, can you revisit a happy memory? If you're doing an Ancestral Activation, can you ask your ancestors to show you a positive Blueprint that you're surrogating? When you're observing your children, can you play detective with their positive attributes? Rather than reading this book and then applying the concept to every tantrum, panic attack and nightmare, can you also apply it to your sunniest family moments?

▷ So, your child loves being in nature ... where did that love come from?

▷ Your kid is super-attached to a teacher ... could they be in their Soul Cluster?

▷ Where did you learn to be so loving, courageous, caring and kick-arse?

▷ Can you join the dots back to your past life joy, as well as to sorrow?

Oh, and let's not forget about all our mediocre lifetimes. The ones where we quietly evolved during mundane moments. When we weren't murdered or burnt as witches. When we led gentle lives of 'normal' contentment. It reminds me of a tongue-in-cheek article

I read about a past life workshop that took place at the Burning Man festival. It was funny, wrote the reporter, that every person there had experienced a past life as a great healer, a pharaoh, a king, or another tragic hero. Nobody was 'just' a mum or 'just' a normal kid. Or, if they were, they hadn't imprinted it on their soul memory.

That's why I wanted to end the book on this important chapter: how can you explore past life wisdom but remain, firmly, in the present? When it comes to all our past experiences, how can we live them, learn from them, and then close the loop so we can find peace in the present and then thrive in the future.

## ▷ Connecting through Joy

A couple of years ago I noticed that I had become a victim to my negative bias—our tendency to place more weight on negative experiences. My husband and I had produced our third baby and, as a new mum again, I felt vulnerable about my self-worth; my attractiveness; my vibrance; what I brought to our relationship. So, I reverted to my teenage coping mechanism—connecting through suffering.

With my husband, I'd open every conversation with bad news. I began to ruminate on memories from my past and talk about them incessantly. I also started to focus on perceived problems in our relationship. One night, during another heavy conversation, my husband said, 'It feels like you're looking for problems.' I replied, 'If we're not talking about our problems, what if we have nothing to talk about?'

That was a lightbulb moment for me. Because of 'everything I've been through', I can easily revert to talking about trauma to fill an awkward silence. It's the downside of the anti-small-talk movement. We say we don't like small talk. We want to 'deep dive' with every person we meet at a yoga class. But, in doing so, our trauma can become a crux. We can use it to bond, or worse, to see it as the best part of our personality.

Once again, this is all about balance. I love that I'm not afraid to tackle difficult topics. I believe that in being open about my past, it will create a more open and authentic dynamic in our home and help my kids to know that they can turn to me with their own problems. No judgement! I don't, however, want it to be our only way to connect. The other day, I heard a contestant on a reality TV show say, 'I taught my kids to survive, but I didn't teach them how to love.' If I hadn't been to therapy, I think my kids could be saying something similar in 15 years' time, 'Mum taught us how to suffer, but she didn't teach us how to celebrate.'

In the past, I have been great at supporting friends through tragedy—I know what to say, I don't turn away—but I've been absent or uncomfortable when they have a 'win' or, even, when it's something as minor as their birthday.

I want to raise my children in a trauma-informed household, one that acknowledges how our past can impact our present, but I don't want it to be the focal point of our family. Nor do I want to see my kids as the sum of their painful past experiences, even if it does help me to put their triggers into perspective.

Whilst writing this book, I went deep into past life theory, including, as you've read, being a guinea pig for past life regression, ancestral healing and re-patterning. But I've also gone a long way in healing my discomfort with joy. This year, I felt safe to really celebrate Christmas for the first time instead of dwelling on the years that my dad had cancer or the final, hideous Christmas with my late husband. For my son's fifth birthday I went all-in on a superhero birthday party, despite being in the process of still healing my hip injury. I chose to celebrate in the moment, instead of dwelling on something that happened yesterday (or yesteryear)!

As you'll know by now, the goal of this book is to really see your children for all that they are, and all that they've been. As it turns out, my research did focus a lot on past life trauma and negative life experiences. But, to really see our children, we must see their whole soul, including the parts that twinkle in the sunlight. Parenting can feel like a series of problems—another snotty nose, another teacher's note, another broken heart—but we also must see, really see, every cosy, comfortable, contented moment when everything feels easy. The evidence we gather will lead us to form a conclusion about our lives and whether we can feel safe in them.

It reminds me of an exhibition put on by The Rubin Museum of Art in New York called 'The Future is Fluid'. Based on Buddhist principles, it took the idea that the future ahead of you is determined largely by what you choose to remember. As part of an art installation, visitors were asked to write two things on a post-it note: their hope for the future and their fear for the future. Their hopes went on a red board and their fears went on a blue board. The idea was that we all have a choice—will you take the 'red pill' or the 'blue pill'? Will you see life as a magical mystery or a fruitless struggle? The visitor statements included:

▷ We are anxious because ...how we live feels like it's rapidly shifting underneath us and we're not exactly sure what will be valued in a few years.

▷ We are hopeful because ...we are the ones we've been waiting for. Unprecedented uncertainty brings unprecedented opportunity for reflection, healing, radical change, and intentional movement forward.

▷ We are anxious because ...the future is uncertain.

▷ We are hopeful because ... through our social fragmentation, the seeds of a hundred new flowers are being sown[1].

This is really the best balance we can aim for, and it's become the overriding final message of this book. To live in trust and create a tuned-in society, we must acknowledge our past, including our collective traumas and the role we have played in them. But we also must acknowledge our in-built wisdom and knowledge, and the capacity we have to create change in the future.

It's similar to a mantra/prayer that, in the early days of parenthood, I had stuck on my bedroom mirror: help me to live from a place of love and not fear. I still try to come back to this statement whenever I face the fears that come with parenting, whether it's my child's first day of school or any of my unfounded worries for our future.

Every day, it can feel easier to cling to our toughest memories because that's what society has trained us to do, but we can push against it, whilst still acknowledging their impact. In the future, I wonder if more children will remember happy past life memories if we can create a culture where happiness is as news-worthy as tragedy. Maybe we can do an experiment together. Create a household where we celebrate as comfortably together, as we suffer. And see if our children's children remember happier memories. Of course, you won't remember this conversation. Or maybe you will ...

## ▷ Goodbye for Now

One of the reasons that I have, in the past, found it difficult to celebrate my children, and my love for them, is because I could already feel my heart breaking in the future. Loss. It's a word that we're raised to fear. Impermanence. We know it's true, but we don't want to believe it.

As I've shared, whilst I was writing this book, I was also working on a TV show about the death of my first husband. It's been an incredible experience, but also extremely confronting. At times,

I've pushed my current husband away because it felt too difficult to have a foot in each world, especially in recreating the moment that I was widowed.

A week after doing the Nun Karma Repatterning process, I started crying during sex with my husband straight after orgasm. When he asked why I was crying, I replied, 'It can feel so hard to love you.' My poor husband didn't ask what I meant for three weeks, until he had the (Dutch) courage to bring up the subject. I tried to explain, 'It just feels so hard to remember that time and then to let myself love you.' Every kiss can feel like something I'll miss when the time inevitably comes for us to part ways.

Exploring past life parenting and integrating it into our life has helped to lessen this fear immensely. In fact, as I edit this book six months after writing it, this fearful version of me feels like a distant memory. It is staggering how much I've changed and grown as a mother, and woman, even since starting this book. I feel freer and bolder and just, well, happy.

For one, there is the belief that we will cluster back with our loved ones again and that we will even remember them on a soul level. I also take comfort from the idea that we've all done this thing called Life before, possibly on multiple occasions. It's like giving birth—once you've done it once, it often feels less scary (unless your birthing experience was traumatic, of course). Well, I believe that I've already died and been born many times. I've already watched my partner die; my parents die and even my children die throughout multiple past lifetimes. So have you, and you have the capacity not only to endure it, but to embrace it.

In this life, when I was 23, I clearly remember when my first husband was dying, hiding in the hospital toilets on the phone to my dad. 'I can't do this,' I cried. He replied, 'Yes you can ... and you will.' Of course, it was true because it's all part of the human experience.

As we come to a close, these are some of the learnings which stand out for me from writing this book:

▷ Our children are so much wiser than we think they are and that's a huge comfort for parents who don't always know the answers.

▷ Your sensitive child is your greatest teacher and healer, especially if we teach them to trust themselves (and us!).

▷ Our souls are bigger than we could ever imagine; our human form is just the surface of our ability to live, love and know.

▷ Healing is a never-ending, multi-dimensional journey, so never give up hope.

▷ There are huge benefits to belief, however that looks for your family.

▷ Looking back is a window to forgiveness.

▷ Everything is a lesson in love.

▷ This is not the end; you'll always get another chance, but let's still give this chance a good go!

Should you believe in past lives and all the wisdom that comes from them? That's not for me to say, even though I've written an entire book on the topic. What I will say is that there has never been a more complex time to be alive (or to raise little humans). The world is moving forward at an astonishing rate, whilst still clinging onto archaic ideas that block our own journey of awareness. We need all the knowledge that we can access to navigate the world, let alone be happy in it.

Before her death, the past life pioneer and hypnotherapist, Dolores Cannon said, 'This is your play. It's all that life is, a play, an illusion. I've had people say that, when they go through the death experience into past life, they look back and say, "It's just a play. I see all the actors on stage getting ready to play their parts. I see all the actors getting ready to come on stage and play their parts. When I was there I took it so seriously but now it's like a blink of an eye."[2]

If we are just the tip of the iceberg of our souls and there is, indeed, a larger part that isn't tethered here, wouldn't it be wise and even fun, to explore it together? Isn't it comforting to know that if we screw this life experience up, albeit with the best of intentions, we get another go?

As I say to my babies at bedtimes on the days that haven't gone smoothly, 'Well, we all did our best, shall we try to be kinder tomorrow?' And tomorrow and tomorrow, and tomorrow ... until eternity. I'm happy to commit to that. Are you?

## Epilogue
# It's Never too Late (The Day I Met My Daughter's Soul)

▷ One of the reasons that I struggle to read parenting books is because I never want to realise too late what I could have done better. Maybe you've even had twinges of this whilst reading this book—the ache of 'what if', which can come when you're shown a new way of parenting after your child has already reached certain milestones.

If this is the case, let this final chapter be a tonic. It's an uncomfortable chapter for me to share, but it's also incredibly important. And it's a gift that I'd love to leave you with.

You'll have noticed that a lot of this book focused on my son, the child who kickstarted my interest in past life parenting in the first place. But, it was a past life activation that involved my oldest child, my daughter, which I come back to, again and again, when I'm craving connection and comfort, and a kick-up-the-butt to remember what matters.

I've mentioned before that I'm a trained Akashic Record Reader—a process in which you can access your Akashic Records, which is supposedly the place where we store memories of our past life experiences. I haven't written much about it in this book, because I didn't want to place myself as an expert. But, during the training to become a reader, I undertook a past life activation. In it, I connected with the soul of my daughter, my beautiful firstborn.

In the activation, I was shown a vision of myself and my oldest daughter, then five-years-old, sitting in chairs, facing each other. I asked her: 'Why are you in my life? What do you need from me?' At this point in my life, I realised that a lot of my focus was on my son—and on myself. I was only just recovering from the depths of sleep-deprivation. I was deep in therapy attempting to heal my own inner child. I was also extremely introspective, staring in on myself instead of out at my children. In my journal, I wrote down the message I received from my daughter's soul. It was this:

*'I want to be your best friend. I want to show you how to be excited by life. How to have friends and be led by joy. How to always feel young. You think it is an ending as I grow up, but it's just the beginning.'*

That all sounds positive, right? But there was another part of the message, which brought a lump to my throat and made me instantly want to reach out and hold my firstborn. The message from my daughter's soul continued:

*'But you've forgotten me. It used to be me and you, and you were so happy. You keep putting layers and layers on me. This can be the beginning of our exciting, fun life together—more exciting than any life you've known. If, and only if, you see me.'*

I didn't have to go too deep to understand the message. I could process it from a place of curiosity, not shame, and still understand it. When I first became a mum, I let myself be happy, but then, of course, my own crushing expectations came into the equation.

More work. More projects. More stuff. More pressure to be both the perfect mother and successful journalist. Over time, I created more layers between us; I could see it.

If I was honest, I sometimes found my daughter confronting. Even at six years old, she seemed to find it so easy to be ... happy. In many ways, my highly-sensitive-son was easier to cope with. He felt like more of a reflection of my personality. Yet, here was my daughter, who could be my greatest teacher, waiting for me to notice her—waiting for me to get over myself. I kept coming back to that message:

*'This can be the beginning of our exciting, fun life together—more exciting than any life you've known. If, and only if, you see me.'*

It might sound like this activation would bring up shame, but it was a revelation. Today, I have this journal entry laminated and pinned above my desk. It's right above my computer screen as I type this. It's a reminder that the greatest inspiration can be right in front of you. Wanting to paint together; to meditate together; to show me how she sees the world. Telling me all about the plants in our garden and asking me if we can go to India to see the elephants. When she was a baby, I'd tell her, 'It's me and you, just us two'—but then I layered the stresses and insecurities of life in between us. In this moment, I remembered the truth of our contract: she and I are here to be a double act, so that she can show me how good life can feel ... when you let it.

Since then, my relationship with my daughter has changed so much, it's almost incomparable. At the age of six, I involve her in all my creative projects. (She is currently brainstorming the name of a children's book that we're writing together.) When I'm feeling down, she is an instant upper for my energy. The confidence of her self-expression astounds me, as does that of her friends.

Recently, I was voice-noting with Justine Sharkie, who has become a treasured friend since I interviewed her for this book. During our virtual discussion, I received a 'download'. I heard a voice in my mind saying, 'When the boys cause instability, the girls are the answer.' It wasn't just about my daughters; it was about the girls of Gen Alpha and younger.

Open your eyes and see them. As the old system and paradigms shake and break down, society's systems break down, the boys will be the ones who struggle more to adapt. Not so much my son's generation, but certainly those older. They're not going to adapt as easily and fluidly. But, the girls are ready; they're ready for change and they're going to be the ones leading the way. Talking in a very dualistic way, the boys may not be able to offer stability as the systems change. But, the answer is the girls; they are wise, and they are ready.

One final anecdote before I love you and leave you ... Recently, when I was sitting in meditation, I suddenly felt overcome with waves of love. Instantly, I knew this love was being sent to me by my daughter, but not in the present day. Somehow I knew that a future version of my daughter—now a fully grown woman—was sending love and healing back to me in that moment. I had to smile; I had taught her well.

As parents, we can feel like the whole world rests on our shoulders, along with the crushing responsibility of our family's happiness. But, our children are searching for ways to remind us about who they are and what they can do.

In the big-soul, big-picture scheme of life, it's not all down to you, their caregiver.

If you take anything from this book, let it be this: there's huge relief when you realise that a parent doesn't need all the answers—and that a child has more answers than we think they do.

Amy x

# Acknowledgements

▷ To all the experts, parents and children who shared their insight and stories with me for this book, thank you for being so generous with your time, your thoughts, your memories, your dreams, and your wisdom. I always went into this book saying, 'I'm not the expert' and you gave me the jigsaw pieces for what became an amazing and surprising picture, which didn't end up looking anything like I imagined.

To my wonderful team at Hay House Australia for believing in this book when it was little more than one paragraph in an email. To Rosie for the whole-hearted yes. To Maggie for the beautiful phone-call that inspired me to go 'all in'.

To my dear friends, Fleur and Justine (the former who introduced me to the latter), thank you for all the voice-notes, the sanity checks and the encouragement, and for cheering me on to dive into this past life experiment. Whilst writing this book, I didn't just complete a manuscript, I discovered two new friendships and I'm eternally grateful.

A special thank you to Meagan for sharing your story when it was so raw. And to Anita for re-opening your story. Both of your experiences will stick with me forever.

To Lizzie, for the many, many walk-and-talks, which I always treasure. I love that we ended up writing books in tandem and going on this rollercoaster together. For the constant reminder to hold my nerve, stay on my path and to not upper limit myself. I love you heaps, my friend.

To my mum, who was the first person to read this book, thank you for your time, your encouragement and your interest. To both of my parents, I'm so grateful that you introduced me to the world of meditation and inner healing. I hope and believe that we've taught each other along the way.

To my sister, Louise, for getting me in a way nobody else does. For the things we say and the things we don't have to explain to each other because we already know.

To my husband, I know this isn't your world, but thank-you for the hours upon hours of talking about past lives, reincarnation and quantum physics. I'm so grateful that we can co-parent from different pasts and rebirth within our relationship together. Our soul recognition class worked, because I knew I loved you as soon as I saw you.

Finally, to my three babies, the inspiration for this book. Mothering you in this lifetime has already been a ride; my greatest challenge and my greatest triumph. Before this life, during this life and after this life, I will always love you. Your Mama Bear. xx

# 10 Ways to Support Your Child's Soul

1.  **Surprised but never shocked.** When your kids come up with statements you didn't see coming, be surprised but never shocked—there is a difference. My kids constantly surprise me, but never shock me.

2.  **Ask gentle questions, but don't expect answers.** Make them feel safe and secure. We can't look at children with our own eyes and expect them to see the world we see

3.  **Don't favour fearless.** Our fearless children can be our favourite children, as they're more convenient. But, get curious about your kid's fear; see it an adventure to unpack them together.

4.  **Share your truth.** When your kids ask if you're sad, tell them the truth, but reassure them. 'Yes, I'm sad, but it's not your responsibility. I'm just having a feeling.' Remember, we don't want to fool their intuition.

5.  **See allergies as an emotional barometer.** Is your child picking up on conflict or something he sees as a threat? Could you set better boundaries for your family?

6. **Nurture their soul friendships.** If your child seems to really see—and be seen–by one of their peers, arrange a playdate, make friends with their parents, nurture those soul relationships. (But, also realise, even soul friendships don't have to last forever.)

7. **Teach them energy hygiene.** Help them sage their bedroom, place cut-up limes beside their bed (thanks, Jessica Lynne!), teach them to move away from troubling energy, politely.

8. **Practise 'the satellite dish'.** My Fave tip fron Dana Childs. Imagine a satellite dish sitting against your body, as if it's resting against your hips or your belly. The energy coming at you hits the satellite dish and is sent back outwards.

9. **Don't make death a dirty word.** Talk about the cycle of life. If you don't know how, open the conversation and be guided by them. (You might learn something.)

10. **Be a cycle starter.** Instead of obsessing over the trauma you don't want to carry forward, think about the cycle of happiness, peace and love you want to kickstart for them.

## 15 AFFIRMATIONS FOR PAST LIFE PARENTS

*There is no stress because there is no fear.*

*I love the creativity of motherhood.*

*My creative mind will always be able to find a solution.*

*We have flexibility and freedom.*

*I love our tribe.*

*My children respect me and each other, because I respect and love them*

*I can stay serene in any situation.*

*Our love and fun only gets better and better.*

*I teach my babies to live judgement free. We are safe.*

*I deserve a joyful baby.*

*I am confident and capable, and perfectly in my feminine power and choices.*

*I choose to love my babies, always and forever, with total ease and joy.*

*I teach my babies how to love, create and care.*

*I'm surrounded by my favourite people and we are supported in every way.*

*This is the height of life.*

# Appendix

▷ This chapter includes a list of recommended resources on past lives, parenting and emotional healing. The best and most up-to-date resources can be found on my website *amymolloy.com.au/ pastlifeparenting.*

There, you'll find a list of useful downloads, templates, and bonuses that will help you make the most of the ideas covered in the book, as well as my Five Step Past Life Parenting Plan—a simple way to put these ideas into action.

## ▷ Past Life Regression & Hypnosis

For an up-to-date list of my recommended past life regressionists and hypnotherapists, visit my website. Please do your own research and take responsibility for finding a therapist who is a good fit for you. I also recommend combining past life therapy with counselling or traditional therapy, especially if you have experienced complex trauma.

## ▷ Akashic Record Readings

I periodically open my bookings for private meditation journeys, which combine akashic record readings, clairsentience, counselling techniques and hertz sound healing. I work with clients to identify their blockages, find the root cause of their stress and discomfort, and move through it with trust and clarity. To see if I have available appointments or to join my waiting list, visit my website, *amymolloy. com.au/ private-meditation-with-amymolloy*

## ▷ Cord-Cutting Meditation

For an audio recording of a simple cord-cutting meditation, which you can listen to for free, visit my website, *amymolloy.com.au/ pastlifeparenting*

## ▷ Nun Karma Repatterning Process

To download the full Nun Karma Repatterning guide, visit my website, *amymolloy.com.au/pastlifeparenting*

## ▷ Witch Wounds Course by Justine Sharkie

To find out more about Justine Sharkie's work and to explore her courses, visit *justinesharkie.com*. You can also find a link via my website *amymolloy.com.au/pastlifeparenting*

## ▷ Psychotherapy Support for Parents

Gidget Foundation Australia is a not-for-profit organisation that exists to support the emotional wellbeing of expectant and new parents to ensure they receive timely, appropriate and specialist care. They offer free counselling sessions to parents, delivered face-to-face or online. www.gidgetfoundation.org.au

## ▷ Suicide Prevention Training

Learn simple steps to support those at risk of suicide by undertaking Lifeline's Suicide Prevention Training. Their basic course can be undertaken in three hours online or they have a more comprehensive two-day training program. www.lifelinesouthcoast.org.au/training/ suicide-prevention-training

> **Core Values List**

As discussed in the chapter, Co-Parenting from Different Pasts. Scan through the below list with your partner and see which values jump out at you. Pick the top five values that call to you and see if your list is the same-same or different. You can also do this with your friends, your parents or your older children. It's an interesting conversation starter!

- Authenticity
- Achievement
- Adventure
- Achievement
- Adaptability
- Alertness
- Altruism
- Authority
- Autonomy
- Balance
- Beauty
- Boldness
- Compassion
- Challenge
- Citizenship
- Community
- Competency
- Contribution
- Creativity
- Curiosity
- Determination
- Fairness
- Faith

- Fame
- Friendships
- Fun
- Fidelity
- Focus
- Foresight
- Fortitude
- Freedom
- Grace
- Gratitude
- Greatness
- Growth
- Happiness
- Honesty
- Humour
- Influence
- Inner Harmony
- Justice
- Kindness
- Knowledge
- Leadership
- Learning
- Love

- ▷ Loyalty
- ▷ Meaningful Work
- ▷ Openness
- ▷ Optimism
- ▷ Order
- ▷ Organisation
- ▷ Originality
- ▷ Peace
- ▷ Pleasure
- ▷ Poise
- ▷ Popularity
- ▷ Recognition
- ▷ Religion
- ▷ Reputation
- ▷ Respect
- ▷ Responsibility
- ▷ Security
- ▷ Self-Respect
- ▷ Service
- ▷ Spirituality
- ▷ Stability
- ▷ Success
- ▷ Status
- ▷ Trustworthiness
- ▷ Welcoming
- ▷ Winning
- ▷ Wisdom
- ▷ Wonder

# About the Author

▷ Amy Molloy is an award-winning journalist, and magazine and book editor, and the writer of the hit podcast, *The Space,* which has more than 7 million lifetime downloads. The founder of LightWriter Media, her work is dedicated to 'words that move the world forward', and finding ways to support bold, brave stories to be written, published and valued.

Amy is the author, editor and ghost-writer behind more than 50 books, including her debut memoir, *Wife Interrupted* and its follow-up, *The World is a Nice Place.* She is also the author behind the children's book, *How to Recycle Your Feelings* (available in English and Chinese translations) and the self-help guide, *Heal Your Story, Change Your Life: 10 Days to Inner Freedom.*

Proud to be a trauma-informed editor, Amy supports women across the world to share their stories through her online course, *The Book Writing Remedy* and LightWriter mentoring program.

Currently, she lives on the South Coast of Sydney, Australia, with her nature-loving husband, and three wild and wonderful children.

*Follow Amy @amy_molloy*
*Amymolloy.com.au*

▷ **15% off The Book Writing Remedy**
▷ *Write a Book Based on Your Life & Take The Fear Out of Sharing Your Story.*

In Amy's bestselling online course, *The Book Writing Remedy*, unlock her proven non-fiction formula for turning your life story into a bestselling memoir or self-help guide.

- ▷ Build your confidence as a writer and get crystal clear on your story.
- ▷ Learn how to set boundaries that respect your private life when sharing your experiences publicly.
- ▷ Stand out from the competitive with insider insight on making your book a commercial sell-out.
- ▷ Learn how to protect the other people in your story, whether it's an ex-lover, family members or your current employer.
- ▷ Make writing about your past a healing experience that helps you to let go and move forward.
- ▷ Access Amy's tried-and-tested book pitching template.
- ▷ And discover how to sell a book before you've even finished writing it. (Yes, it's very possible—our writers have proved it!).

As a reader of *Heal Your Story, Change Your Life,* you can get **15 per cent** off the price of joining *The Book Writing Remedy.* Just enter the code HEAL at the checkout at *amymolloy.com.au/ bookwritingremedy*

## ▷ Praise for The Book Writing Remedy

'Writing a book can be a lonely experience. With Amy as your editor, you won't feel alone. She really cares about you and your story.' – Fleur Chambers, author of *Ten Pathways* and *Wholehearted Confidence*.

'My publishing deal wouldn't have been possible without her support, guidance and belief in my story — a very tough story to tell.' — Meagan Donaldson, author of *Still a Mum*.

'Having someone bolster your confidence and give you the direct feedback you need is invaluable. I have no hesitation that, without Amy's experienced guidance and support, my first published book may still be a notion rather than hitting the shelves.' – Doctor Kate Luckins, author of *Live More with Less*.

'Amy's writing and editing genius, and holistic book coaching were like having a secret weapon onboard. Every time I wanted to scream, "Stop the ride", Amy kept me on track, through writing and editing the book, to publishing it and beyond.' – Lizzie Williamson, author of *The Active Workday Advantage*.

'I can't recommend Amy's writing course or 1:1 sessions more highly—she is a gifted, talented writing coach who has your back as an aspiring author.' – Tehla Jane Bower, author of *A Mother's Space*.

# References

## Chapter 1: Generation Reincarnation

1   Children who report memories of past lives, Jim Tucker, University of Virginia website, accessed March 2023, https://med.virginia.edu/perceptual-studies/our-research/children-who-report-memories-of-previous-lives/

2   The Past Life memories of children with Jim Tucker, online video, accessed March 2023 https://www.youtube.com/watch?v=igR7wZG_paI&t=145s

3   Alex Gurley, These Parents are convinced their children have had past lives, and their stories are eerie, Jan 2021, accessed March 2023, https://www.buzzfeed.com/alexgurley/parents-convinced-their-children-have-past lives

4   Parents, what spooky past life memories did your kid utter? Reddit, accessed September 2024. https://www.reddit.com/r/AskReddit/comments/mkru9p/parents_what_spooky_past_life_memory_did_your_kid/?rdt=62873

5   Ian M Giatti, Most Americans believe in karma, over 25% believe in reincarnation, December 2022, accessed March 2023, https://www.christianpost.com/news/87-of-americans-believe-in-at-least-one-new-age-belief-poll.html

6   McCrindle, Faith and belief in Australia: a national study on religion, spirituality and world view trends, May 2017, accessed March 2023, https://mccrindle.com.au/app/uploads/2018/04/Faith-and-Belief-in-Australia-Report_McCrindle_2017.pdf

7   Eli Somer, Journal of Loss and Trauma, Beliefs in Reincarnation and the power of fate, September 2011, accessed March 2023, https://www.researchgate.net/publication/232859614_Beliefs_in_Reincarnation_and_the_Power_of_Fate_and_Their_Association_With_Emotional_Outcomes_Among_Bereaved_Parents_of_Fallen_Soldiers

8   Deena Prichep, Adopting a Buddhist ritual to mourn miscarriage, abortion, August 2015, accessed March 2023, https://www.npr.org/2015/08/15/429761386/adopting-a-buddhist-ritual-to-mourn-miscarriage-abortion

9    Josh Kimball, Father of reincarnated world war ii pilot says Christian faith undeterred, June 09, accessed March 2023, https://www.christianpost.com/news/father-of-reincarnated-wwii-pilot-says-christian-faith-undeterred.html

10   The Past Life memories of children with Jim Tucker, online video, accessed March 2023 https://www.youtube.com/watch?v=igR7wZG_paI&t=145s

## Chapter 2: Better than Google

1    3 year old recalls past life, identified killer, May 2014, accessed March 2023, https://www.indiatoday.in/world/asia/story/3-year-old-remembers-past-life-identifies-killer-location-of-body-193650-2014-05-20

2    Michael Armstrong, Reality bending things kids say, TikTok post, November 2021, accessed March 2023, https://vt.tiktok.com/ZS8b7EJBY/

3    Emma Elsworthy, Curious children ask 73 questions per day, December 2017, accessed March 2023, https://www.independent.co.uk/news/uk/home-news/curious-children-questions-parenting-mum-dad-google-answers-inquisitive-argos-toddlers-chad-valley-tots-town-a8089821.html

4    Justine Sharkey, interview with Amy Molloy, March 2023, Zoom.

5    Mind Body Green podcast, The Science of Past Life Memories w. Jim Tucker, accessed March 2023, https://podcasts.apple.com/au/podcast/the-mindbodygreen-podcast/id1246494475?i=1000518021622

6    Philippe Rochat, Five levels of self-awareness as they unfold early in life, Emory University, Feb 2003, accessed March 2023, http://psychology.emory.edu/cognition/rochat/Rochat5levels.pdf.

7    David the Medium, original interview with Amy Molloy, Zoom, March 2023.

8    Gillian Mohney, The science behind when and why children lie, April 2016, accessed March 2023, https://abcnews.go.com/Health/science-children-learn-lie/story?id=38066555

9    Jim Tucker, Advice to parents of children who are spontaneously remembering past lives, accessed March 2023 https://med.virginia.edu/perceptual-studies/resources/advice-to-parents-of-children-who-are-spontaneously-recalling-past-life-memories/

## Chapter 3: Triggers & Glimmers

1    Chrissy [remaining anonymous so no surname], interview with Amy Molloy, Instagram, March 2023

2    The Science of Past Life Memories with Jim Tucker, Mind, Body Green Podcast, accessed April 2023, https://podcasts.apple.com/au/podcast/the-mindbodygreen-podcast/id1246494475?i=1000518021622

3    Phobias in Children Who Claim to Remember Previous Lives, Ian Stevenson, Journal oJScientific Exploration. Accessed April 2023, https://med.

virginia.edu/perceptual-studies/wp-content/uploads/sites/360/2016/12/STE34Stevenson-1.pdf

4    Eli Bliliuos, interview with Amy Molloy, Zoom, March 2023.

5    Concerns about Hypnotic Regression, Doctor Ian Stevenson, University of Virginia, accessed April 2023, https://med.virginia.edu/perceptual-studies/resources/concerns-about-hypnotic-regression/

6    Jim Tuckers, Advice to parents of children spontaneously remembering past lives, accessed March 2023, https://med.virginia.edu/perceptual-studies/resources/advice-to-parents-of-children-who-are-spontaneously-recalling-past life-memories/

7    Breaking cycles and reparenting yourself with Dr Becky Kennedy, We can do hard things, podcast, accessed April 2023, https://podcasts.apple.com/au/podcast/we-can-do-hard-things-with-glennon-doyle/id1564530722?i=1000579281486

8    Ian Stevenson and cases of the reincarnation type, Jim B Tucker, Journal of Scientific Exploration, accessed April 2023, https://med.virginia.edu/perceptual-studies/wp-content/uploads/sites/360/2015/11/REI36Tucker-1.pdf

9    Circle of Security International, What's the Circle of Security? Accessed March 2023, https://www.circleofsecurityinternational.com/circle-of-security-model/what-is-the-circle-of-security/

## Chapter 4: Autonomy & Personal Freedom

1    Rebecca Maklad, interview with Amy Molloy, February 2023, Zoom

2    King Tut tomb babies 'possibly' his twins, ABC Science, September 2008, accessed March 2023, https://www.abc.net.au/science/articles/2008/09/02/2352885.htm#:~:text=Tutankhamen's%20tomb%20containing%20the%20mummified,been%20stored%20at%20Cairo%20University.

3    Ashley Hämäläinen, Instagram, accessed March 2023, https://www.instagram.com/p/Ci_KBBwADXG/

4    Sarah Jane Perman, Instagram, accessed April 2023, https://www.instagram.com/p/ChmmU5SKW9J/

5    What your baby can't tell you, Janet Lansbury, accessed March 2023, https://www.janetlansbury.com/2010/04/what-your-baby-cant-tell-you/

6    Dana Childs, original interview with Amy Molloy, Zoom, March 2023

7    Jonathan D Lane, The roles of intuitive and informants expertise in children's epistemic trust, Child Dev, May 2016, accessed March 2023, https://www.ncbi.nlm.nih.gov/pmc/articles/PMC4428962/

## Chapter 5: Soul Clusters & Chosen Families

1   Bernadette (no surname as remaining anonymous). Interview with Amy Molloy. Instagram, March 2023

2   Toni Reilly, 7 Signs your child has been your mother in a past life, TikTok, accessed April 2023, https://www.tiktok.com/@soullifezone/video/7172393667888532738

3   Doctor Brian Weiss, We have many soul mates, Mega institute for holistic studies, Youtube, accessed April 2023, https://www.youtube.com/watch?v=nghslLSwkSs

4   Mothers' recognition of their newborns by olfactory cues, M Kaitz 1, A Good, A M Rokem, A I Eidelman, accessed April 2023, https://pubmed.ncbi.nlm.nih.gov/3691966/

5   Eli Bliliuos, interview with Amy Molloy, March 2023, Zoom

## Chapter 6: Big Feelings & Real Meanings

1   Peter Smith, interview with Amy Molloy, March 2023, Zoom.

2   Four reasons why people become empaths, Judith Orloff, June 2017, accessed March 2023, https://www.psychologytoday.com/au/blog/the-empaths-survival-guide/201706/four-reasons-why-people-become-empaths-trauma-genetics

3   Justine Sharke, interview with Amy Molloy, March 2023, Zoom

## Chapter 7: What Did We Sign Up For?

1   Volition, Sayadaw U Silananda, published by Inward Path Press, accessed April 2023, http://www.buddhanet.net/pdf_file/volition.pdf

2   Sex, desire and our karmic experience, Sawami Tripurari, accessed April 2023, https://swamitripurari.com/2002/07/sex-desire-and-our-karmic-experience/

3   Chakras 7 year development cycle, Malavika, accessed April 2023, https://hellomalavika.com/2012/09/22/chakras-7-year-development-life-cycles/

4   Development of a child's chakra energy, psychologically astrology, accessed April 2023, https://psychologicallyastrology.com/2019/09/20/development-of-a-childs-chakra-energy/

5   What is epigenetics? Centre on the developing child, Harvard university, accessed April 2023, https://developingchild.harvard.edu/resources/what-is-epigenetics-and-how-does-it-relate-to-child-development/

6   Do you carry the trauma of your ancestors? Sara Amare, accessed April 2023 https://bsj.berkeley.edu/do-you-carry-the-trauma-of-your-ancestors/

## Chapter 8: Attachment & Trust

1   Anita Kaushal, interview with Amy Molloy, over email, March 2023,
    https://podcasts.apple.com/au/podcast/slo-mo-a-podcast-with-mo-gawdat/
    id1508914142?i=1000526976508
2   Brene Brown, the anatomy of trust, Supersoul sessions, November 2021,
    accessed April 2023, https://brenebrown.com/podcast/the-anatomy-of-trust/
3   Brene brown on Vulnerability and power, Under the Skin with Russel
    Brand podcast, accessed April 2023, https://open.spotify.com/
    episode/3kvhIaxTbKSZvZ2y0tC6iK
4   Caring for a terminally ill child, Cancer.net, accessed April 2023, https://
    www.cancer.net/navigating-cancer-care/advanced-cancer/caring-terminally-ill-
    child#:~:text=You%20might%20want%20to%20protect,the%20changes%20
    in%20their%20bodies.
5   Faith in a time of crisis, Bryan Goodman, American Psychological Association,
    May 2020, accessed March 2023, https://www.apa.org/topics/covid-19/
    faith-crisis

## Chapter 9: Tweens, Teens & Transitions

1   A Third Of Parents Feel Awkward Talking About Periods During
    Coronavirus, Study Finds, Alice Broster, Forbes, October 2020, accessed
    April 2023, https://www.forbes.com/sites/alicebroster/2020/10/07/a-third-
    of-parents-feel-awkward-talking-about-periods-during-coronavirus-study-
    finds/?sh=578f71d01453
2   Over 20% of parents won't talk to their kids about sex: poll, Emily
    Lefroy, NY Post, June 2022, https://nypost.com/2022/06/16/
    over-20-of-parents-wont-talk-to-their-kids-about-sex-poll/
3   Patterns of Spiritual Connectedness during Adolescence: Links to Coping
    and Adjustment in Low-Income Urban Youth, Anna W. Wright, Joana Salifu
    Yendork, and Wendy Kliewer, June 2018, accessed April 2023, https://www.
    ncbi.nlm.nih.gov/pmc/articles/PMC6246777/
4   With their own voices, The Centre for Spiritual Development,
    November 2008, accessed March 2023, https://www.search-institute.org/
    wp-content/uploads/2018/02/with_their_own_voices_report.pdf
5   Helping your teenager discover their spirituality, Larry Forthun, University of
    Florida, accessed April 2023, https://edis.ifas.ufl.edu/publication/FY1228

## Chapter 10: Standing Out & Fitting In

1   Sometimes even a 3-year-old justs wants to fit in with the group, Duke
    Today, May 2021, accessed April 2023, https://today.duke.edu/2021/05/
    sometimes-even-3-year-olds-just-want-fit-group

2    Childhood Gender Nonconformity and Children's Past life Memories,
Marieta Pehlivanova, Monica J. Janke, Jack Lee and Jim B. Tucker, Division
of Perceptual Studies, Department of Psychiatry and Neurobehavioral
Sciences, University of Virginia School of Medicine, Charlottesville, Virginia,
USA, 4 September 2018, accessed April 2023, https://med.virginia.edu/
perceptual-studies/wp-content/uploads/sites/360/2020/04/4Childhood-
Gender-Nonconformity-and-Children-s-Past life-Memories.pdf

## Chapter 11: Healing Timelines

1    Feeling the Feelings my ancestors never felt, Sah D'Simone and Vir
McCoy, accessed April 2023, https://podcasts.apple.com/au/podcast/
the-spiritually-sassy-show/id1547752940?i=1000611446526
2    ALOK: What makes us beautiful? What makes us free? We can do hard
things with Glennon Doyle podcast, accessed April 2023, https://podcasts.
apple.com/au/podcast/we-can-do-hard-things-with-glennon-doyle/
id1564530722?i=1000552537690
3    The bravest conversation we've had: Andrea Gibson, Glennon Doyle,
We can do hard things, accessed June 2023, https://open.spotify.com/
episode/3VkAIbTrJxat8IOAY1GXYP
4    Why Glennon says we should all be in recovery, Glennon Doyle, We
can do hard things podcast, accessed April 2023, https://podcasts.
apple.com/au/podcast/we-can-do-hard-things-with-glennon-doyle/
id1564530722?i=1000609422964

## Chapter 12: Co-Parenting from Different Pasts

1    Overcome rejection in this past life regression, Toni Reilly TikTok,
accessed April 2023, https://www.tiktok.com/@soullifezone/
video/7143732835009006849
2    Letters from Esther #36, Esther Perel, accessed
April 2023, https://www.estherperel.com/blog/
letters-from-esther-36-fighting-with-your-partner-about-values
3    Sam Harris: On death, Big Think, YouTube, accessed May 2023, https://www.
youtube.com/watch?v=d_Uahu9XNzU

## Chapter 13: Parenting without Shame

1    Almost two thirds of mums have felt shamed over their parenting choices,
The Cut, June 2017, accessed April 2023, https://www.thecut.com/2017/06/
mothers-parenting-shame-criticize-survey-michigan.html

2   Nun Karma. A Free Open Source Re-Patterning Formula created by Carol
    Cannon, Gail Glanville, Kathie Joblin, Nancy Martin, Carolyn Winter, Helene
    Zahn-Chilberg.

3   Cognitions in Sleep: Lucid Dreaming as an Intervention for Nightmares
    in Patients With Posttraumatic Stress Disorder, Brigitte Holzinger, Bernd
    Saletu, and Gerhard Klösch, august 2020, accessed April 2023, https://www.
    ncbi.nlm.nih.gov/pmc/articles/PMC7471655/

4   Lucid dreaming: an age-dependent brain dissociation, Ursula Voss 1, Clemens
    Frenzel, Judith Koppehele-Gossel, Allan Hobson, European sleep research
    society, 2012, accessed April 2023, https://pubmed.ncbi.nlm.nih.
    gov/22639960/

5   Why children have more control of their dreams, Ann Lukits, Jan 2013,
    accessed April 2023, https://www.wsj.com/articles/SB1000142412788732446
    8104578246013675170372

6   Lucid Dreaming Tutorial For children And Young People (Or Parents),
    Stefan Zugor, Youtube, accessed April 2023, https://www.youtube.com/
    watch?v=rA4DiXrUhxk

## Chapter 14: The Relief of a Timeless Life

1   Mo Gawdat, What happens after death? Youtube, accessed March 2023,
    https://www.youtube.com/watch?v=lwtg5f8cGuU

2   Psychic medium Laura Lynn Jackson and Dr Mark Epstein, video, accessed
    March 2023, https://www.youtube.com/watch?v=I7oJ67l_N_Q

## Chapter 15: Living for the Future

1   A Monument for the anxious and hopeful, Rubin Museum,
    accessed April 2023, https://rubinmuseum.org/events/
    exhibitions/a-monument-for-the-anxious-and-hopeful

2   Dolores Cannon, Instagram, accessed June 2023, https://www.instagram.
    com/p/CtfLDR4shqw/?hl=en

 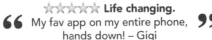

We hope you enjoyed this Hay House book. If you'd like to receive our online catalog featuring additional information on Hay House books and products, or if you'd like to find out more about the Hay Foundation, please contact:

Hay House LLC, P.O. Box 5100, Carlsbad, CA 92018-5100
(760) 431-7695 or (800) 654-5126
www.hayhouse.com® • www.hayfoundation.org

———

*Published in Australia by:*
Hay House Australia Publishing Pty Ltd
18/36 Ralph St., Alexandria NSW 2015
*Phone:* +61 (02) 9669 4299
www.hayhouse.com.au

*Published in the United Kingdom by:*
Hay House UK Ltd
1st Floor Crawford Corner,
91–93 Baker Street, London W1U 6QQ
www.hayhouse.co.uk

*Published in India by:*
Hay House Publishers (India) Pvt Ltd
Muskaan Complex, Plot No. 3,
B-2, Vasant Kunj, New Delhi 110 070
*Phone:* +91 11 41761620
www.hayhouse.co.in

———

**Access New Knowledge.**
**Anytime. Anywhere.**

Learn and evolve at your own pace
with the world's leading experts.

www.hayhouseU.com